Queensland Geographical Journal ...: Including The Proceedings Of The Royal Geographical Society Of Australasia, Queensland ..., Volume 19...

James Park Thomson, Royal Geographical Society of Australasia. Queensland Branch, Brisbane

CONTENTS.

———

VOL. XIX.

SUGGESTION.

Every person desirous of bequeathing to the Society any money is requested to make use of the following

FORM OF BEQUEST.

I give and bequeath to the Honorary Treasurer for the time being, of the ROYAL GEOGRAPHICAL SOCIETY OF AUSTRALASIA, QUEENSLAND,

the sum of ....

....

for the benefit of the said Royal Geographical Society of Australasia, Queensland, to be expended as the Council of the said Society may deem expedient for the promotion of Geographical Science or the purpose of exploration in Australasia.

N.B.—All Donations presented to the Royal Geographical Society of Australasia, Queensland, are acknowledged by letter and in the JOURNAL OF PROCEEDINGS.

NOTE.—All Communications should be addressed to the Hon. Secretary, at the Rooms of the Society, Brisbane, Queensland.

Queensland

Geographical Journal.

No. 5. New Series. 1904. Vol. XIX.

THE MYSTERY OF ANCIENT OPHIR.*

By the Hon. F. T. BRENTNALL, M.L.C.

Our subject opens to our review remote periods of history. It supplies interesting materials for archæological reflections and investigations. It suggests important historical comparisons. It sheds a side-light upon a wide-spread system of ancient religion, known by the term of litholatry—the worship of stones of a particular shape. It takes us to a region which has passed through many forms and conditions of occupation; through many phases of civilisation; but which, through all its variations of production, and all its vicissitudes of domination, has maintained its reputation as a vast and prolific producer of gold It exhibits to our observation an extensive series of mysterious ruins, which have been a wonder and a problem for centuries. At different periods during the last 500 years those ruins have astonished travellers, soldiers, and missionaries. Often have the questions been asked:—Whose hands piled up these immense structures? For what purposes were they built? For forts intended to protect men and precious property? Or, For temples for nature-worship?

There cannot be any doubt about the golden wealth of the region formerly known as Monomotapa. Numerous Portuguese authorities asserted this at a time when Portugal had the run of the entire country. Portuguese missionaries stationed themselves in some of the important centres of the country. Had Portugal been a colonising power the whole of the territory now known as German East Africa and British Rhodesia might have belonged to that country. But, with our traditional British pride, may we not say that a better fate awaited it? Perhaps it is to the credit of Portugal that in the

---

* Read before the Royal Geographical Society of Australasia, Queensland, 19th October, 1903.

16th and 17th centuries its rulers were more eager to win the Kaffirs to the faith of the Catholic Church than to subjugate them and seize their territory.

In the archives of the Propaganda of the Faith in Rome there is a letter from Lisbon, dated June 28th, 1631; in which is the following:—"The kingdom of Monomotapa is very large and full of people; nearly all pagans, and without knowledge of religion. It is rich in gold mines, ebony, and ivory. And in the opinion of many it is the ancient Ophir, where Solomon sent his ships which sailed through the Red Sea to the coast of Africa. A very easy navigation and full of ports. In this kingdom the Portuguese hold possession of many places near the sea, and an immense number in the interior. I shall commence with the city of Sofala, which beyond the Cape of Good Hope is the first we find inhabited by Christians. It is a fortress of the king of Portugal, governed by a Portuguese Hidalgo, subject to the Governor of Mozambique."

In those sacred archives are many important letters bearing on the condition of the people, and on the forms of government prevailing in south-eastern Africa, two or three centuries ago. Since then many travellers have gone, for various objects, to those interesting districts. By some of them wonderful stories were told of splendid ancient ruins, which led the imagination back to periods and conditions of occupation now lost in the haze of antiquity.

The first exciting flush of interest in the Titanic ruins of the ancient empire of Monomotapa led to exaggerated conceptions of their character and objects. That period of sensation has passed away, but a certain fascination still invests the subject. The period of calm investigation has come. This is an age when investigators desire and aim to get at the origin of material things, and at the beginnings of all history; an age of scientific research. There are not many new countries to be explored, so scientists dive into the depths of remote history. Able men devote their lives to the interpretation of the signs and symbols of ancient sacred worship, and of the hieroglyphic records of worn-out national life and history. Especially are they eager to search out all that can be discovered concerning the sayings and doings of peoples whose supremacy among their contemporary nations has for ever passed away. Nations which lived their day, made their display, then lost their power and glory.

One of those decayed nations was Phœnicia, a small maritime country on the shores of the Mediterranean Sea. This insular power was in the brilliant zenith of its glory about 30 centuries ago. What Great Britain is to the commercial intercourse and the maritime relations of the world now, Phœnicia was to the international trade and traffic of the age when Hiram was king of Tyre, and David and Solomon were successive kings of the land of Israel. On this point

we may quote from a book written by the Hon. A. Wilmot, the following:—"The history of the people of Phœnicia, to whom we trace
the litholatry exhibited in ancient monuments on the shores of the
Mediterranean, in the fertile country of Arabia, and amidst the
ancient gold-mines of South-eastern Africa, is a study of absorbing
interest. What the great British Empire is to the 19th century
Phœnicia was to the distant ages when Solomon's temple was built
at Jerusalem, and Hiram, king of Tyre, sent out expeditions to the
distant shores of India, Arabia, and South Africa."

It is in those ancient historical annals of the Hebrews, which
the religious belief of many peoples has invested with a superior
sacredness, that we find the most precise, explicit, and reliable references to some region of enormous wealth, which then was designated
"Ophir." Was Ophir the name of a specific and exclusive locality
or country? On this point opinions differ. Most of the earlier
critics were agreed that it was some particular locality, or region,
where gold could be easily obtained. In Dr. Smith's "Dictionary
of the Bible" we read that it was:—"A seaport or region from
which the Hebrews in the time of Solomon obtained gold." The
erudite article which thus begins names three or four countries on
which conjecture expended itself. These were Armenia, Arabia,
India, Africa, and many arguments are cited in favour of each
hypothesis. One writer quoted in that article allowed that there
might have been two Ophirs; one in India, the other in Arabia. In
the interesting book written by the Hon. A. Wilmot, who was com-
missioned by Cecil Rhodes "to make the best researches in his power
in the archives and libraries of Europe with the object of discovering
all possible traces of the history of Monomotapa, the land which is
marked 'rich in gold' on the maps of the 16th and 17th centuries;
also of the great Zimbabwe ruins which have been brought to notice
almost sumultaneously with the conquest of the country in which
they are situated," the author says:—"Ophir was a generic title for
a rich commercial country, used in the same way as 'Tarshish.' The
latter name we know was given to more than one place; so there may
have been an Indian as well as an African Ophir. The former would
be on the Malabar coast; the latter was inland from the Sofala coast,
in South-east Africa (Monomatapa)."

A preface to this book was written by Mr. Rider Haggard; he
says:—"Within the last thirty or forty years Baines and other
travellers, now dead, reported the existence of great ruins in the
territories known as Matabeleland and Mashonaland, and on the
banks of the tributaries of the Zambesi River, which, from their
construction, must have been built by a race of civilised men, and
in 1871 Herr Mauch re-discovered the fortress-temple of Zimbabwe,
that now, as in the time of the early Portuguese, was said to be

nothing less than the site of one of the ancient Ophirs." Here again we have the idea of more Ophirs than one.

Gold is inseparably associated with, the designation "Ophir." The gold of Ophir was renowned for quality as well as quantity. King David, in the last days of his life, inspired by reverent regard for the temple and worship of Jehovah, gave out of money which he held by his own right, 3,000 talents of gold for the adornment of the sacred structure which his son Solomon was to build. The nobles of his kingdom also contributed 5,000 talents of gold. According to one authority the talent of gold contained 2,750 ozs.; so that the 8,000 talents handed to Solomon for his great building contained 22,000,000 ozs. Truly the precious metal was plentiful in those days! And somewhere, within navigable distance of Palestine, there must have been a vast auriferous region whence that gold came. During the reign of David's successor it continued to come. Always the region, whence it was obtained, was designated "Ophir."

It is only in recent years that we have had definite and confident statements by competent travellers that the Ophir of the Phœnicians and Hebrews was in South-eastern Africa. With most of the old writers it was a matter of conjecture and surmise. Even the larger British Encyclopedias dispose of this important subject in a few sentences. It should not have been either too trivial or too abstruse for a contribution to the Encyclopedia Britannica. Thomas Baines, a British geographer and artist, was early in the field of exploration. His book, "The Gold Regions of South-eastern Africa" was published in 1877. Since he called attention to the stupendous evidences of mining on a gigantic scale at some remote period of the world's history, many intrepid travellers have gone on his tracks. One after another have endorsed his convictions; till now it has become an accepted fact that, no matter where other Ophirs may have been, nor how many of them, the principal source of supply of gold for Tyre and Jerusalem was Africa.

But for the sacred books of the ancient Hebrews the account of one of the most interesting periods of human history would be shrouded in the impenetrable mists of antiquity. Thanks to those narratives, and to the historian Josephus, we know that when king David was in the prime of life Hiram ascended the Tyrian throne and soon became his friend and adviser. After the death of David the alliance continued with Solomon for twenty years. It was an alliance of mutual service and interest, as well as of friendship. Many of the subjects of Hiram were men of the sea; expert mariners. Solomon owned the famous port of Ezion-geber, on the Red Sea; which was made by him a mart of commerce and a harbour of navigation.

In I Kings ix, 26-28th verse, we read :—"King Solomon made a navy of ships in Ezion-geber, which is beside Eloth, on the shore of the Red Sea, in the land of Edom. Hiram sent in the navy his servants, shipmen that had knowledge of the sea, with the servants of Solomon. And they came to Ophir, and fetched from thence gold—420 talents, and brought it to King Solomon." This navy made triennial voyages, and always came back richly freighted with gold, silver, gems, birds, valuable odorous timber, and apes. In the next chapter we find an amazing statement :—"Now the weight of gold that came to Solomon in one year was six hundred threescore and six talents of gold." Although outside these Hebrew records we have not much confirmation of these statements, they cannot be treated as legends. We must accept the fact that there were millionaires in those days.

The commercial eminence of Tyre was no less renowned than its voluptuous nature-worship. Mr. Wilmot writes :—"Luxury fostered the love of gold, and all that could gratify the desires of a sensual people. Now, more than ever, were immense efforts made by the most skilful mariners, miners and colonists of antiquity. Arabia was treated as the pivot, or point of departure, and Ophirs of the southern seas were opened to the world. It is probably to a period shortly before the establishment of the large Tyrian commercial relations with Ezion-geber that we may trace the first visit of Phœnician Nature-worshippers to Monomotapa, where they built the colossal edifices whose remains now stand sphinx-like for explanation."

It would, did time permit, be worth while to bring within tangible vividness some indisputable evidence that this conclusion is not without foundation. One of the most reliable of recent explorers is Theodore Bent, whose book entitled "Giant Cities of Mashonaland," is now a standard. After describing "The Great Zimbabwe" in the territory of the British South Africa Co., between the Zambesi and the Limpopo. he contends that the buildings were erected by people who practised the nature-worship of Phœnicia. On many stones the phallus is realistically, or conventionally represented, while numerous towers and pillars are of the same character.

In passing it may be instructive and interesting to consider the real meaning of the astounding figures found in the Bible, relating to gold. They sound almost like a fairy-tale. The mind does not readily comprehend what is meant by a yearly income of 666 talents of gold. It means 1,831,500 ozs. Truly a royal revenue! It is very nearly as much as all the miners at Gympie have got in 19 years; more than all the Rockhampton district, Mt. Morgan included, has produced in 11 years; more than the great Charters Towers field has yielded in four years. All the goldfields of Queensland during the years 1901 and 1902 did not produce so much gold by 135,494 ozs. as one year's income of King Solomon. As the gold of Ophir is always described as "fine," we may compute its value at £4 per ounce. This would give that renowned monarch an annual income of £7,326,000. It sounds like fiction—like an inflated legend of some old story-teller. But the records of ancient Judaism are not composed of romances.

Where was Ophir? While a lot is said about the good things that came from that place, nothing is said definitely about its geographical situation. This is a remarkable omission. Its location is a hoary mystery; a riddle of thirty centuries. When the pomp and magnificence of Solomon disappeared, and the rival factions of the nation, after his death, indulged in civil strife rather than maritime commerce, the mists of oblivion seem to have begun to gather over the region from whence that luxurious king had drawn the material elements of his splendour.

What conjectures and surmises have been indulged—what theories and hypotheses have been invented—about the interesting problem of the source of the gold and gems which contributed so profusely to the regal opulence and renown of the most affluent and voluptuous of all the Hebrew Kings! Whither went those fleets which triennially made voyage to some distant and unfailing El Dorado? From what perennial source came the precious metals, the dazzling gems, the gorgeous birds, the ornamental feathers, the superior timber, and the grotesque animals, which gratified and enriched a monarch whose reputation for wisdom, and whose renown for opulence and splendour had been circulated far and wide?

These are questions which, for many centuries, have puzzled the brains of antiquaries and philologists. A place of so much maritime and commercial importance must have a history, however obscure. Where are the records? The sublime poetry of Ezekiel, which describes the downfall of Tyre, says nothing of the mysterious source which contributed so substantially to the power and grandeur of that small kingdom. Where was the secret of lost tablets and inscribed parchments to be found? Many able men have tried by conjecture, by cupidity, by research, to locate the fascinating region. They have recognised the probability of gold still being found there. But the problem could not ever be solved by archæological investigation in schools and academies. The search had to take another form; had to be made by hardier methods; to be consummated amid more substantial evidences. Not by leisurely pursuit of thought on tracks of philology and theoretical conjecture could this riddle be solved; but by tiresome exploration on the tracks of miners who have slept the sleep of the dead for ages. Wherever the Ophir of Bible history was, there must have been extensive mining.

Mining, especially deep-mining, leaves palpable evidences in mounds of excavated debris, tangible proofs and monuments of large industry. Surely also, where masses of toiling men have annually turned out gold and silver by millions of ounces there ought to be relics of human habitation, and remains of public buildings. Naturally also one would expect that mausoleums would be found where the dead workers were buried.

Many travellers have gone in search of Ophir. It is their narratives which interest us now. We are not much concerned with the derivation of the word Ophir; nor with the fine-spun theories of academic philologists about the meaning of the word, or the place to which it referred. This is not a matter of fable or fabrication. It is a question of fact to be settled on the spot

On the eastern side of the continent of Africa, laved by the everlasting surges of the Indian Ocean, the most valuable stretch of coast line has for four centuries been in the possession of the unenterprising Portuguese race. There has been a deplorable lack of colonising genius. How different might have been the condition of South-eastern Africa if that door of entrance had been in the keeping of the race which, more than all others, has displayed a genius for colonising, and for wise, amicable, and honourable dealing with the native races of any country which it has secured by discovery, or acquired by conquest. By what are called "Concessions" Great Britain has secured rights of access to central Africa of a most valuable kind. From Beira on that coast runs the railway to Mashonaland, which forms a part of that extensive and fertile territory which now, through the sagacity and enterprise of one of Britain's noblest sons, bears his worthy name "Rhodesia"; and for the good alike of England and Africa is painted red on modern maps. About 150 miles further north is Chinde, at the entrance of the mighty Zambesi.

Dr. Peters says:—"As England gained a foothold in Beira by the Mashonaland Railway Concession and a customs treaty, which gives goods destined for the British hinterland duty-free transit through Portuguese territory; so in Chinde—the actual harbour of the Zambesi—England has procured for herself an exceptional position through the so-called 'British Concession.' The navigable Chinde estuary was discovered by an English officer, and the Zambesi was thus opened up to modern navigation." From this port, on Easter Monday, A.D., 1899, Dr. Peters and his party started up the Zambesi on a search for ruins and riches. It was a quest worthy of a dashing explorer.

A few days afterwards he wrote in his diary:—"For years I had had certain fantastic ideas about Fura. This time, for once, the reality far surpassed all my fancies. Anything more picturesque, and at the same time more mysterious, even the fancy of a Rider Haggard could not have depicted, than the entrance into this an-

cient and fabulous Eldorado. Like two rock castles the masses of
slate stood on the left and right of the Muira River, overgrown on
the top by a dense growth of green. Below the waters of the river
rippled, reflecting the dark blue sky of the tropical world. Before
us a river valley opened, into which, on both sides, the dark rock
walls descended; at first like waves of hills; then steep and wide;
and above this charming landscape lay a sinister silence of death;
Sabbath stillness, as it prevails in the tropics at midday. Thus did
I find the eastern entrance to Fura, on Saturday noon, April 15th,
1899." In this extract there are three noticeable expressions: "Fura,"
"Masses of slate," "Fabulous Eldorado." Already the glow of hope
has kindled the enthusiasm of the explorer for auriferous country.

At many points of his subsequent journeyings he gives us glimpses
of beautiful scenery. Here is one:—"These mornings on the African high plateaux represent the finest weather one can imagine;
a bright air plays around hill and veldt; the atmosphere becomes
transparent; every sound is distinctly heard. The light is like that
of a sunny September day in England, but much more intense. Light
and shade are sharply contrasted. The eye penetrates for an immense
distance; and, above all this splendid manifestation of Divine great-
ness the dome of the sky is extended deep and wide; with a beauty
which the poor inhabitant of the north has no chance of seeing at
home. The Italian blue sky is dim compared with this radiant bril-
liancy. Dewdrops sparkle on grass and trees like millions of pearls
and diamonds, for a light hoar frost is spread over the landscape.
Towards seven o'clock the burning sun-ball rises higher, and absorbs
all these jewels with which Queen Night has decked the earth. A
march amid such surroundings is better than all the luxuries of Europe, and fully repays all the worries and exertions of African travel."

But we are told of other things besides natural scenery. He
sojourned in the region of diversified zoology, where animals of mons-
trous structure abounded. He tells us of the ferocious alligator,
the repulsive crocodile, the ungainly hippopotamus. He points us
to a group of chattering monkeys, or a family of baboons. He writes
of the stealthy panther, the pretty but treacherous leopard, the roar-
ing monarch of the forest; of giraffes, bisons, elephants. Besides
these were sundry flocks or herds of lesser game; sport for the rifle,
or food for the travellers.

But the main object of Dr. Peters was something more practical,
more substantial, more serviceable, than admiring scenery, or shooting game, or studying zoology. His was not the exclusive mission
of the geographical explorer. He gives detailed descriptions of the
topography of the country; he describes, with the touch of a literary
artist's hand, some of the exquisite scenery through which he passed;
he occasionally grows enthusiastic about the foliage on the banks of the

majestic rivers, the grandeur of massive mountain scenery, the fantastic shapes into which the magic hand of nature has formed huge upheavels of mountain granite; for example: "The country now became extraordinarily rich in water; rivulet after rivulet runs from the eastern margin straight through the valley towards the Ruenje. A schist mass rose on the eastern side; the west was still granite in fantastic shapes and forms. We could turn again to contemplation of the landscape, which had become most charming, particularly on the western side, where the granite still continued to cheat one's fancy. There, big and distinct, rising from the rock, the figure of a knight with mantle and sword stood, hand on hilt, gazing over the wide valley at his feet. When we approached nearer, the stony head was as the head of a skeleton. The likeness was so deceptive that Herr Gramann and I stopped for a moment, not knowing whether we had a trick of nature or a work of art before us. Around him the usual caricatures and forms of fantastic pinnacles and rocky castles fronted us." Dr. Peters was really after the discovery and acquisition of mineral properties rather than the excitement and pleasure of travel. He was curious to see the most marvellous and interesting remains of a lost civilisation about which the haze of mystery hung, but more eager to find the sources of the precious metals about which ancient history tells such marvellous stories.

Gold has always had the fascination of the most precious of metals. Men make sacrifices for any object that is fascinating. For gold they will submit to hardship and privation, to sacrifice and suffering. No danger terrifies them; no obstacle deters them; nothing, but absolute failure disheartens them.

What the splendour of precious gems is to the Moguls and Rajahs of India in this age the glory of gold was to the Pharoahs and Kings of ancient history. It was the emblem of majesty and the evidence of wealth. The 10th chapter of 1st Kings is like a fairy tale out of Oriental romances. So abundant was gold that silver was of no account. King Solomon drank wine out of golden goblets, lifted his meat off golden plates, washed his hands in golden ewers, rested his foot on a golden footstool, and made his songs and proverbs by lights standing in golden candlesticks. In that luxurious age silver was of no account because of the profusion of the better metal. But gold is no product of fairy fancy, nor of magician's wand. It never was, never will be, got without risk, trouble and enterprise. In spite of the obstacles which often lie between the gold-seekers and the deposit of the metal, there always have been, there always will be, men prepared to take the trouble.

When we have steamed up the Zambesi with Dr. Peters we may gaze in reflective amazement on the pathetic ruins of an effete civilisation which long ago retired from business, and left stupendous evi-

dences of its industry to perish under the intense natural elements
which prevail in equatorial Africa. We look with startled bewilder-
ment on the remains of massive works reared ages ago by hands
which have utterly disappeared from human sight or discovery. The
enormous ruins of their work are visible; but the workers have vanished into an undiscoverable oblivion. Were it not for those ancient
annals of a surviving race which has a vitality far superior to its
instinct of nationality, annals which have been preserved because of
human faith in a God whose supreme will and wisdom are believed to
control human destines; modern explorers would have found it difficult to link that dead past of ingenius and gigantic structure with any
phase of remote life, or with any section of ancient nationality.

While our traveller was in the district of Inja-ka-Fura one me-
morable noon-day one of his party entered his tent, in a condition
of suppressed excitement, and said:—"I have good news. I have
seen the ancient ruins." During the afternoon of the same day Dr.
Peters and Mr. Gramann visited the spot. This was what they saw.
"Round the margin of a hill appeared the remnants of an old cyclopean wall, the stones of which had apparently been worked with
a pick, as they showed certain triangular forms with the edges turned
outwards. Far back from the margin, towards the centre of the hill,
we found a mighty horizontal ledge, which we first took to be the
entrance to a cave. Later researches proved this was a mistake.
Round this ledge a wall of stones, that were artificially shaped, in
the form of a heart, had been built. Near this wall we found a
great number of curiously formed stones which I am inclined to regard
as betylæ, which were objects of religious worship in the oldest Semitic cults. Among these betylæ I found a phallus. Phallus-worship
was connected with the original Semitic sun-worship. That these
stones are the work of man, and not the sports of nature, is proved
by the fact that they are formed of sandstone, while the rock and
the whole formation of the hill is crystalline slate. We had little
time in that afternoon to study this find. Before everything I wished
to examine the cyclopean wall which intersects the middle of the hill,
which Puzey had seen from below. We therefore broke a new way
to the north of our ascent; across vast debris once more; which lay
in stupendous heaps on the edge of the precipice. About thirty feet
below the hillside we discovered a sort of court-yard, and had the
wall before us; which in a mighty circle, following the outlines of
the hill, stretches to both sides. Here it stood fifteen feet and higher;
there it was half broken down; there broken down altogether. At
some places the stones stood bare; at others overgrown with a dense
vegetation. Reverence and awe filled us as we stood spell-bound
before these relics of a remote civilisation. . . We were both over-
powered by the historical significance of what we saw; and we were

thrilled with the mystery of a past whose years were numbered in thousands."

For what object were those great buildings erected? For the abodes of workers?—or the stores of wealth?—or forts of protection! They could not have been built solely for temples of worship; nor wholly for theatres; nor for purposes of art and culture. They were too plain, massive and practical. They do show evidence of the stone-cutter's work, and of the builder's skill. They conform exactly with Phœnician work found in other parts of the world. They were shaped and fitted with expert skill for some definite and permanent purpose. No mortar was used. When they ceased to fulfil their primary object; when or why they were abandoned, we know not. The ruins are there; but no elucidating records. We are in a region where scope has to be given to surprise and surmise; to reflection and conjecture.

We seem to be compelled to join in the consensus of modern opinion that these colossal ruins are relics of that golden age when the Hebrew king of peace surrounded himself with all the luxurious contributories to Oriental life and splendour; when a host of expert handicraftsmen were engaged in setting gems, and shaping and chasing gold from the affluent sources of Africa. The ancient names of Solomon and Hiram will, for all time, be associated with the golden age. Between that remote period and this there have been national developments, aggressions and disruptions; dynastic revolutions; rising and falling of empires; the prominence and the disappearance of nations that once flourished in the pride, power and prestige of undaunted bravery and majesty; the rising of new nationalities whose barbaric origins have vanished into the mystery of the unrecorded past. Was it the enervation of the divided monarchy of Israel which led to the decline of the mining industry in the African Eldorado?

We cannot follow Dr. Peters into all the details of discovery and argument by which he strives to connect Solomon, Hiram, and the ancient Egyptians with the gold regions of East-Central Africa. He succeeds to his own satisfaction. Nor can we closely pursue his track of travel. The ruins of old cities and mining works abound. Here is one account of ruins that appear to have been found in Kaiser Wilhelm's Land. Laid out on some definite plan were ancient walls; some in quadrangular shape. Terraces ran round a hill, one wall above the other. These ruins gave a vivid impression that they were the remains of ancient dwellings. Below the buildings were hundreds of heaps of stone similar to those they had been seeing for weeks past; all artificially filled with debris of quartz. Dr. Peters says:—"It was clear that we stood here on the field of former activity, but now the silence of death lay over the landscape. . . Bewildered, and brooding over the mysteries of our surroundings

we went on, crossing the eastern escarpment by a pass. Over and
over again mysterious groups of stones were passed. . . Very
often walls stood in a circle, like the mouths of our wells, built of
schist or granite, and filled with rocks of another kind. Again and
again we encountered quadrangular and round stone walls, evidently
the remains of human dwellings. . . In the afternoon I explored
the settlement more carefully. In the centre stood a large quadrangular building, 24 feet long and 7 feet wide. On the left-hand
side, in front, were five circular walls; to the right of these, directly
in front of the house, were a number of the characteristic stone-heaps
of quartz, as we had seen them throughout the morning, I had two
of these opened, as the thought had struck me that they might be
perhaps ancient burial-places. Gramann, who controlled this exca-
vation, stated that the quartz at the bottom had been subjected to
great heat, and he took the holes in which the debris was lying to
be a kind of stove, which might have served to prepare the quartz
for crushing. His theory seemed to receive a certain confirmation by
the fact that behind the main house were three washing dishes, cut
into the rock, inclined to the one side, with a small margin on the
lower side, which might have been used to wash the crushed quartz.
A strong round-house into which wound a spiral path, protected on
both sides by a wall, was the strangest of those ruins. This house,
we thought, might have been the treasure house. We had, then,
here the dwelling of the mining engineer, with houses for the boys,
distinct traces of quartz that had been worked by fire; dishes for
washing the crushed quartz, and a treasure-house on the bank of a
running water-course."

The party pursued their journey. They had not proceeded far
before they came upon more remains of ancient civilisation. A laby-
rinth of stone buildings. A mountain-side along the face of which had
been cut "a gigantic system of artificial terraces." The doctor writes:
"Underneath this terraced mountain we found a number of old stone
walls; it took more than an hour to march through them. At the
northern end of the ruins I found a circular building, which had
apparently been a place of worship. Exactly opposite the east stood
an altar of stones, on both sides of which stood five smaller altars com-
pleting a circle. Here, again, we found the artificially formed curious
stones which we had found on the height of the Fura ruins; among
others I found again a Phallus. The strangest feature was a road
bordered by stones, which in manifold mysterious windings led from
the western side towards the temple. Might this road have served
the purpose of processions? I had no answer to this and many other
questions which rushed upon me, and in a sort of bewildered restless-
ness I wandered through this tangle of apparently unsolvable rid-
dles."

Dr. Peters declared that from the beginning of his South African enterprise he had decided to extend his explorations at least as far as the Sabi River. To him the very name of this river suggested the Hebrew epoch of South African history. From the Sabi and Lundi rivers the traveller is beckoned onwards by the chain of ruins first explored by Bent, whose most brilliant example of ruins is found to the east, in the so-called Zimbabwe, near Victoria Falls. Dr. Peters writes in his journal :—" On April 3rd, 1900, I arrived at Umtali in order to prepare for my Sabi expedition. Fifteen days later, after crossing the mountain torrent Nyamyaswi, no less than eighteen times, the party camped 3,450 feet above sea-level. They passed a beautiful waterfall. The next day the picturesque views on the Umtali warmed his enthusiasm. He wrote :—"The mountain sides rise ruggedly often with fine effect, on both sides of the river. The bright colours of sycamores and other trees glow on the mountains. Then come whole strips full of Euphorbia, palms, and bananas. The mountain chains are split up in places into picturesque cones and domes 6,000 to 7,000 feet high. Then again the glowing red slate forms whole fortresses, with turrets and platforms. Fancy grows alive. One imagines one has entered the kingdom of legend, and passed into the fairy world itself." On this journey he had shooting practice at big game. He describes a visit from a lion and how he killed it.

But we are concerned with gold, not with game. Dr. Peters insists that the theory that Solomon's gold came from India is discredited because no traces of old gold mines have been found there. " No chain of ruins are there which lead one to suppose that a prehistoric mining population once dwelt there." But in South Africa he finds " indisputable geological proof of one of the richest and most extensive gold formations existing on our planet. Here many thousands of old mines have been found which were sunk to a depth of 50, 150, 400, 600, 900 to 4,000 feet, and from which millions of tons of gold must have been extracted. This chain of ancient gold mines stretches from the north of the Zambesi to the Murchison Mountains in the Transvaal, from Gorongoza and the Lower Sabi to beyond the Hunyati, and as far as Bechuanaland to the west. Here, at last we find the ancient ruins; whole cities, fortresses, and temples, estimated to number 500; characterised by the civilisation of the Himyarites of South Arabia, and by the symbols of the ancient worship of Baal-Ashera. ' What other country in the whole world can enter the lists in the face of these facts? ' "

It is impossible for us to follow Dr. Peters through all the arguments by which he has reached the conclusion that South-eastern Africa was the Eldorado of the ancients. But before closing our references to those arguments we must make one or two important extracts. In the recapitulation of his researches and discoveries he says:—" On the Zambesi we found the old half-fabulous district of Fura again, with its ancient ruins, which plainly showed that they formed part of the old Semitic sphere of civilisation. The wall round the middle of the hill, the betylæ, the phallus that I found by chance, are typical of Punic buildings. Round those ancient ruins, from which the figure of Baal looks down on us across thousands of years, lives the Makalanga nation, which in its worship of the Kabulu Kagore has preserved the old Semitic natural religion until the present day. Here, as thousands of years since, sacrifices are still made to Baal on the hills and heights, fire-worship is still practised, and stones are still objects of veneration. Simultaneously, mining of the precious metal has gone on here steadily from the time of the ancient pioneers, and still continues."

He then recounts the discoveries of the ruins of Inyanga, which he says:—" Tower like a note of interrogation written by some vanished and forgotten hand. Among the ruins of the Inyanga valley all travellers have noticed, as I did, the remarkable pit-like buildings sunk in the earth, walled in with cyclopean stones and provided with covered side-passages."

Our last extract is an important one: The Doctor says.—" Let us make a final summary. It is shown that in South Africa, far back in the second thousand years before Christ, a Himyaritic colony existed. It is shown that the great temple of Zimbabwe was built about 1100 B.C., that is, about a century before the allies of Solomon sent ships to Ophir. The Sabeans, allies of Solomon, were predominant here at that time. It is shown that throughout this whole region gold was mined on a large scale at that time, but that precious stones, copper, and tin were also obtained here. All the other products of the Ophir voyages—ivory, apes, indiarubber, and guinea-fowl were also obtainable here.

But our task is not quite finished. We have not quite done with Dr. Peters. Looking closely at some of his envious references to the large possessions of the British in South Africa; and at his rueful contrasts of the British and German methods of colonisation, it is not difficult to perceive the gall in the ink with which he writes. In his opinion German methods are too timid and conservative. They have no " go " in them. They are selfish and exclusive. He likes the British open-door policy better. But he cherishes no amicable feelings towards the British. To him they are restless, crafty, greedy aggressors; willing, if permitted, to gobble up all the territory of the earth. He applauds their pushful and adaptative skill; beyond that he has little that is good to say of them. He would infinitely prefer that those splendid territories which he so graphically describes, with their fertility of soil, their variety of scenery, their majestic rivers, their stores of mineral wealth, were owned by his own Fatherland. He is specially aggrieved that the grand territory, known as "Rhodesia" should, by the amazing foresight, the keen and prompt alertness, the broad-minded patriotism, of one of Britain's noble and courageous sons, have passed for ever into British possession. It was, I believe, owing largely to this same traveller that the section of African territory at the back of Zanzibar, which precludes the line of communication between the Cape and Cairo being "all red" as Cecil Rhodes desired, became German.

When the last journey of Dr. Peters and his party through the Sabean territory was ended his reflections were these.—"Interesting to me personally in this my last African enterprise is the fact that the regions traversed were the object of my first colonial scheme. When, in 1883, I began to associate myself with the colonial question in Germany, I handed the foreign office a petition in which I proposed to take possession of this part of South Africa for Germany. The scheme was coldly received by the German Government, because the 'countries south of the Zambesi are regarded as belonging to the British sphere of interest.' This was six years before Cecil Rhodes received his charter for Matebele and Mashonaland. . . Also the German Colonial Society turned its back on "youthful" projects of this sort. How much grander would the position of Germany have been in Africa had it begun by laying hands on the cool, well-watered gold regions south of the Zambesi! The annexations further north could have been added with ease. A German Colonial Empire from the Limpopo to the Upper Nile, and the Gulf of Aden was possible, whose southern frontier would have had, not the English but the Boers as neighbours. At one blow we would have possessed a country for settlers, and in the gold mines a field for the employment of German capital."

Rhodesia! Envy of the nations! Triumph of colonising genius! Monument of a world conqueror, who with small help from Imperial arms or Imperial diplomacy, by will-force and money-force, overcame the racial enmities of some of the fiercest warriors of Africa. Expansive exemplification of the inventive brain of a man whose schemes and projects were so stupendous, and whose success was so marvellous, that his countrymen were amazed, while their empire was enormously extended. If Dr. Peters found the German Foreign Office unsympathetic with his scheme for the acquisition of the territory between the Limpopo and the Zambesi, in the same decade Cecil Rhodes found the British Colonial Office hard to convince that the same areas would be a valuable accession to the British Empire. But his invincible will-force conquered. What has it meant? That a territory equal in extent to British India has been secured: That in a few years, towns grew up, as it were out of the earth; population was attracted by liberal mining and land concessions; the principle of self-government was adopted; a railway was rapidly constructed from the Transvaal to Bulawayo, connecting the Cape, via Kimberly, Mafeking, Tati, with Bulawayo; a journey from Capetown to the northern terminus occupying four and a-half days.

In drawing to a conclusion let us, as briefly as possible, summarise the conclusions reached by the German Explorer. His last search for gold began in April, 1900. His objective was the Sabi River. "The mere name of this river," he says, "suggests the Hebrew epoch of South African history. Here we actually come to the hinterland of the ancient port of Sofala, which has long been regarded as the chief harbour of the Ophir region." He started from Umtali, a British town, on April 13th, 1900. He returned on May 25th. He expresses his satisfaction thus:—"What interesting impressions we had obtained on this journey! To form a clear opinion about South Africa, considered as an ancient Eldorado, one must regard the Sabi chain of copper mines as the necessary complement to the gold mines of Mashona and Manica lands. We can now establish, that gold, copper, and iron certainly, possibly also precious stones, have been worked from time immemorial in this part of the earth. We had already known whence came the gold for the temple of King Solomon. Our journey to the Sabi had by personal observations provided us with a sign-post by which we could perhaps find an answer to the question: From whence did the Egyptians obtain the copper of their voyages to Punt?"

At Umtali Dr. Peters saw fresh memorials and relics, in newly-discovered paintings and sculptures. There were figures much resembling those on the tablets and stones of ancient Egypt, which convinced him that in old times relations subsisted between Mashonaland and Egypt. He sums up results thus:—"My travels between the Zambesi and the Sabi cover a period of exactly two years, and I look back on this space with a feeling of gratitude. Not only was I permitted to reach the practical ends which I had set before me, the opening up of the gold formations of Fura, the acquisition of the Manica gold mines, the examination of the copper workings on the Sabi, fall into this section of my task; but I also think that I am able, in connection with the researches of others, to form for myself a definite judgment upon the mysterious Eldorado of the remotest of human civilisation. On the banks of the Zambesi and the Ruenje, in the mountains of Manicaland, on the tablelands of Inyanga and Melsetter; in one word, among the ruins of a prehistoric and antique mining industry, more sure evidences towards the solution of this riddle are to be found than in the libraries of Leipzic, Berlin or Oxford."

I would now ask you to consider, for a few minutes, the marvellous transformations of history which this subject suggests. When the after-glow of ancient Egyptian glory still threw its charm over the wondrous land of the Nile; when Babylon was in the zenith of its power; when the navy of Tyre, manned by Hiram's seamen, made regular voyages to Sofala, on the east coast of Africa, and returned laden with gold, silver, gems, brilliant birds, costly timber and apes, the alleged ancestors of man; who, and what were the inhaitants of those small islands lying off the north-west coast of Europe? Who will describe to us the rude semi-barbaric conditions of their rough and nomadic lives? The cult of their rudimental religious credulities? The occupations of their hands? The aims and pursuits of their intellect? Did any Druidical vates predict that in those isles lay the embryo of a nation which should dominate the course of the Nile from its rise in equatorial Africa, to its debouchere at several mouths into the classic Mediterranean? Which should, by the indomitable enterprise and the masterful energy of its emigrant nation-builders win, by the diplomacies of peace or the arbitraments of war, the territory of boundless wealth in Central Africa from which Solomon drew the accessories of his glory nearly 3,000 years ago?

We, sons of the old sea-rovers, have with millions of voices lustily sung "Britannia rules the waves." But it seems to be the destiny of Britain, and another section of the Anglo-Saxon race who, by unkindness, were driven out of her empire, to rule most of the fairest and richest portions of the solid earth. They owned and opened up the golden stores of Australia, California, Vancouver, Klondyke. For the last decade they have been opening up the marvellous auriferous deposits of Witwatersrand, and as the fruit of a deplorable war that source of fortunes has come under British rule. And those diamond fields of Kimberly: Is that where the precious stones came from which composed a dazzling portion of the magnificence of which we read in the Hebrew annals of King Solomon's reign? To me, may I say to us? the word Imperial has no repugnance; the noun Empire stands for a glorious history and a glorious destiny. I have faith in that destiny.

DRAYTON AND TOOWOOMBA—THEIR EARLY HISTORY.*

By JAMES TOLMIE, M.L.A.

The first visit of the Royal Geographical Society to Toowoomba seems a fitting opportunity to withdraw from the oblivion in which they have become enshrouded a few of the facts associated with the formation and the progress of the "Queen City" of the Darling Downs, which is giving every indication of becoming in a not very distant future the finest city in inland Australia. It is not, however, possible to treat of the early days of Toowoomba without associating with them the development of the still older town of Drayton, which, from the light thrown by historical research, appears to have been doomed to but a short career of importance. There are still living in our midst men and women whose memories carry them back a long way in the direction of the early beginnings of both Drayton and Toowoomba, and from them I have had frequent opportunities of gleaning reminiscences of a highly interesting nature, which might lend a charm to a paper of this kind. But since my desire is to produce something of scientific value, which may be preserved in the annals of the Geographical Society, I have been careful to abstain from the use of any information to which a suspicion of legendary or traditional character might attach, and have tried to bring under your observation historical facts based on State papers, and on the reports contained in the newspaper Press of that early period—the "Moreton Bay Courier" and "Darling Downs Gazette"—circulating in what was then known as the nothern districts of New South Wales, and now as the southern districts of Queensland.

A discussion which took place in the New South Wales Council on the 3rd Sept., 1854, and was published in the "Moreton Bay Courier" of the 23rd Sept., gives the first account of the manner in which the town of Drayton came to be established, and as there is some divergence of opinion concerning the reason of the choice of the particular site it is desirable that short extracts from the debate should be given without drawing any deductions, since the manner of the foundation is not disputed.

Speaking in the Council, the Rev. John Dunmore Lang, the father of democracy in Australia, who at that time represented Stanley, which embraced the whole of the present Moreton districts, in the New South Wales Council, moved for the production of papers

---

* Read before the Royal Geographical Society of Australasia, Queensland, at Toowoomba, October 30, 1903.

containing the correspondence which had passed between the Government and the Survey Department on the subject of the township of Drayton. Addressing himself to the motion, he said: "The country between Drayton and Warwick was one of the most magnificent he had ever passed over, and was evidently destined to support at some future date a very large population, although at present occupied solely for pastoral purposes. It was in this way the Downs through their length and breadth were exclusively occupied at the present time. To these districts the presence of population, and the creation of wealth attracted adventurers in various departments of the mercantile world. About ten or twelve years ago an adventurer of this description arrived on the Downs, and planted himself at a place called Bomba, on one of the great runs of the Darling Downs, as he conceived, at a sufficient distance from the occupants of the squatting station. He was ordered off by the gentleman owning 220 square miles of station property, and went to a gap in the range, ten miles away from the nearest station. He was again ordered away by another squatter. A gentleman in occupation of one of the stations, which he had since disposed of, pointed out to him a gully that occupied a sort of intermediate position between three of the great stations in that part of the country (Eton Vale, Westbrook, and Gowrie.—J.T.), and had a small waterhole. In despair of getting any better locality to fix himself down upon, he settled himself in this spot, which had since become the present town of Drayton, and there disposed of his wares. A mechanic's hut and a sly grog shop were soon set up, and these were followed by an hotel. Much antipathy was shown by the neighbouring squatters, but those who had erected houses petitioned the Government to lay out a township, which was done; but the allotments as surveyed differed from those applied for. The waterhole which was the first inducement to settlement dried up, and great difficulty was experienced in getting water. The township should have been at a spot where the roads from the south, east, and west converge (Toowoomba.—J.T..). Now this point was some considerable distance from Drayton, in a place where there was some level ground sufficient, and plenty of water available, and which the Government would have selected for the township if they had duly considered the wants of the people, and looked with a prospective eye to the future of the country. He would recommend the removal of the township, as had been done in the case of Gundagai, and to pay compensation to those who had erected houses, out of the 'Waste Land Fund.' A vote of £200 was passed by the Council in 1851 for the construction of a reservoir at Drayton, and a similar sum was contributed by the people themselves, but the expenditure was in vain. Although there was a far preferable spot at a short distance the people were condemned through the act of the Government to locate themselves in this gully, and to subject themselves to many inconveniences. He concluded by asking the Government to lay upon the table of the House the correspondence which had passed between the Government and the Survey Department on the subject of the township of Drayton."

Mr. Campbell seconded the motion.

Mr. Morris, Liverpool Plains, supported it because he believed it was impossible to imagine a more unsuitable site for a town than that in which Drayton was built, and the mistake was the more glaring inasmuch as four miles from the present township an excellent site could be found (Toowoomba.—J.T.).

Mr. H. Stuart Russell (partner with Mr. Jas. Taylor in Cecil Plains.—J.T.), "though not opposing the motion, would show that the allegations of the honourable and reverend member—that the first settlers in the township of Drayton were forced as it were into their position—were incorrect. Though the reverend gentleman in his tour had visited some of the shepherds' huts, he had never heard of him calling at the residences of any of the squatters, and therefore it was to be presumed his information was of a one-sided character. He (Mr. Russell) had been in the district twelve or thirteen years, and therefore knew the facts of the question. The adventurer who had first settled in the township had pitched upon the gully in question because two roads met there (Eton Vale and Cambooya roads, as will be seen on reference to the plan.—J.T.), and it was therefore the most eligible site for a public house, and by which and the store he set up he made considerable money. When the honourable and reverend member for Stanley alluded to the spot beyond Drayton being a more desirable site, because some roads passed there, he should have borne in mind that those roads were not in existence at the period of the first formation of the town, but were subsequently formed by the squatters of the district."

"The Colonial Secretary, in declaring his intention to lay the papers upon the table of the House, in deference to the remarks of Messrs. Morris and Russell, said he thought it was desirable measures ought to be adopted to remove the town to a more suitable site. As to the adventurer who had been referred to, and who appeared to have made a fortune in the place, he did not think his case should be taken into consideration in any subsequent proceedings."

The correspondence asked for by Dr. Lang was laid upon the table of the House, and it is replete with interest relative to the early days of the two townships.

The first of the correspondence is a letter from Mr. E. Deas Thompson, Colonial Secretary to Mr., afterwards Sir, T. L. Mitchell, written on the 4th Sept., 1848, just six years prior to the date of the discussion in the Council. The letter is as follows :—

Sir,

As it appears from a report received from Mr. Commissioner Rolleston that a number of persons are establishing themselves on the so-called township of Drayton, in the district of Darling Downs without license from the Crown, I am directed by his Excellency the Governor to draw your attention to this subject in order that you may have an early opportunity of causing a township to be marked out in that locality, and bringing the allotments to sale.

The present instruction will not, however, extend to those allotments of land which have been occupied under proper authority by inn-keepers, storekeepers, etc., for other than pastoral purposes, previously to the taking effect in the Colony of Her Majesty's Order in Council of 9th March, 1847.

I have, &c.,

(Signed)   E. DEAS THOMPSON

The next paper is a memorial from "Eighteen inhabitants of Drayton," squatters and others, in which the memorialists, among other matters, declare :—

"That the town sprang up naturally, and the inhabitants from local knowledge chose the best site, and that £3,000 had already been spent in Drayton in the erection of stores, inns, etc.

"That the land in the vicinity is of excellent quality, and if allotted in areas not exceeding 50 acres for farms would meet with a ready sale.

"That the memorialists solicit that the chief town of the northern part of the Darling Downs district be fixed at Drayton."

On the 8th May, 1849, the Surveyor-General wrote to the Colonial Secretary, informing him that early opportunity would be taken to lay out a township at Drayton, and submitting an enclosure from Mr. J. C. Burnett, the surveyor in charge of the northern districts of New South Wales, forwarding a plan of Drayton, a photographed copy of which I am able, through the courtesy of Messrs. A. A. Spowers and Hugh MacIntosh, of the Queensland Survey Department, to submit to the inspection of the ladies and gentlemen here present. Following is the enclosure :—

Camp near Drayton,
24th February, 1849.

Sir,

In compliance with the instructions contained in your letter of the 7th September last, No. 48,337, I do myself the honour to forward herewith a plan of the ground at Drayton, showing the buildings which have been erected there.

2. The private buildings which may be considered of value are the inns of Messrs. Meehan and Horton, and the stores of Messrs. Alford, Handcock and Lord.

3. These parties with the exception of Mr. Lord all occupied under license, and have expended considerable sums in permanent improvements.   Mr. Lord only built recently, and of course without authority, and at a much less outlay than the others.

4. The remainder of the buildings are not of much importance.

5. A well recently sunk affords a supply of water sufficient for the present inhabitants.

Mr. T. L. Mitchell,   I have, &c.,

Surveyor-General,   (Signed)   J. C. BURNETT.

In a letter dated Sydney, 8th June, 1849, and signed W. Elyard, Junr., the Colonial Secretary conveys to the Surveyor-General His Excellency's approval of the plan of Drayton, prepared by Mr. Burnett, and asks that a copy of the plan be forwarded to the Bench at Drayton.

An interval of more than three years passed before there was any further correspondence with the Survey Office at Sydney concerning either Drayton or Toowoomba. When it does take place, the suitableness of the Toowoomba site as a place for a township is stated in no uncertain terms by Mr. Assistant Surveyor Moriarty, who writes to the head of his Department in the following strain :—

Drayton, September 1st, 1852.

Sir,

Before proceeding to lay out any more farm allotments on that part of the Drayton Reserve called the Swamp, I consider it my duty to inform you that I believe the object of the parties who have purchased land there, and who are applying to purchase it, is not with a view to agriculture, but with the hope of being able to form a township in opposition to the Government one at Drayton. Were a township to be formed there, I have no hesitation in stating that I believe not another allotment would be sold in Drayton.

The Swamp possesses many advantages for a township which Drayton does not. The soil is exceedingly rich, the ground level, and there is abundance of water, and the finest timber for building. Drayton on the contrary is built on a number of ravines, and ridges, and possesses no permanent water.

I have the honour, therefore, to request that you will inform me, whether I should lay out any allotments on the Eastern side of the water-course at the Swamp for parties wishing it, and, in general, whether it is the practice of your Department to lay out allotments for parties on any portion of a reserve where they may select them.

I have, &c ,

(Signed)   E. O. MORIARTY.

Sir Thos. L. Mitchell,
    Surveyor-General.

The following reply was received :—

Surveyor-General's Office.
Sydney, 26th November, 1852.

Sir,

In reference to your letter of the 1st September last, wherein you inquire whether you should lay out any allotments on the Eastern side of the water-course, at the Swamp Drayton, for persons who are wishing to purchase, I have to request that you will make a design for laying out, and measure and mark out some allotments of one and two acres, in the situation referred to, preserving ways of access, and forward to me a plan and descriptionn thereof, in order that the wishes of the public may be met in this matter.

I have, etc.,
S. A. PERRY,
Deputy Sur. Gen.

Assist. Sur. Moriarty.

This embraces the whole of the correspondence asked for by the Rev. Dr. Lang, and establishes the fact that the design of the town of Drayton was prepared by Mr. J. C. Burnett in the last months of 1848, and the first month in 1849, and the existing township was confirmed in February and May of the latter year. A glance at the photograph of the design shows that Mr. Burnett had to lay out his design without relation to the cardinal points, in order to meet the exigencies of the situation as disclosed by the location of the existing buildings in positions best suited to the requirements of business, or other considerations affecting the welfare of the owners. If the theory advanced by Mr. H. Stuart Russell be correct—that the adventurer who founded Drayton located himself at a point where two roads met, then from the design prepared by Mr. Burnett we may with some degree of certainty assume that the first settler in Drayton was Mr. Meehan, whose inn and probably store is located at the Spring, close to the intersection of the roads from Eton Vale and Cambooya. None of the old families whose names appear on the design have now representatives living in Drayton. The Police Paddock Reserve still remains the Police Paddock, but is never used for its original purpose. The Court House, sold two years ago to the Drayton Shire Council as a recreation hall, is now situated close to where Horton's Inn formerly stood, and which is now converted into a private residence, and is occupied by Mr. Lynch.

The first survey of allotments in Drayton was made by Mr. Burnett in February, 1850, when four sections of town allotments and two suburban sections were marked and submitted to sale on the 31st July, 1850, at Drayton the prices fixed being £8 for town allotments, and £3 for suburban. Of these, twelve town allotments were sold, the purchasers being Eliza Lord, William Horton, M. Meacham, S. Smith, Arthur Hodgson, D. Barry, and E. Dolan. One suburban allotment was sold to Mr. T. B. Yates.

From the records of the Survey Office, it would appear that Toowoomba is an older township in the sense that a survey was made there before the one in Drayton. This survey was carried out by Mr. Burnett in April, 1849, and embraced twelve portions on the west side of the West Swamp, extending from the Black Gully to the neighbourhood of South Street. These were in area from 27 to 40 acres each, and were termed suburban allotments, presumably suburban to Drayton, since the site of the present capital of the Downs was at this period and for many years after known as the "Swamp" in general conversation, as well as in all official documents. Consequently what is now known as the West Ward, and extending in the South Ward as far south as South Street, marked in red on the plan submitted, is the oldest portion of Toowoomba, though until recent years it is the portion which has made least progress, presumably because with but few exceptions the allotments remained unsubdivided. Six of these portions were offered for sale at Brisbane on the 10th October, 1849, at 40s. an acre, but no offer was made for them. They were re-submitted to auction on the 9th October, 1850, when

two portions were purchased by Mr. William Horton. of Drayton.
These two portions are readily discernible on the plan. They are
now south of Russell Street, though at that time no such street
existed. When the Street was first opened it went by the name of
Farm Road. Mr. Horton subsequently sold his portions to Mr. Jas.
Taylor, and Clifford House now stands on a part of one of them.

The interest attaching to the laying out of the towns of Drayton
and Toowoomba is of sufficient importance to warrant a short biogra-
phical notice of Mr. James Charles Burnett, who carried out the
work. He was the son of Mr. William Burnett, of Burnettsland,
Hunter River District, and was born in Scotland in 1815, the year in
which Waterloo was fought. He came to New South Wales with his
parents, and entered the Public Service in 1834 or 1835. He was
chosen for his ability by Sir Thomas Mitchell to continue the survey
of the Dividing Range from Hanging Rock Northward. He commenced the work in October, 1841, and traced the range to about
the 30th parallel, and thence made his way to Brisbane, in September,
1842. Subsequently he was engaged in surveys on the Richmond and
Clarence Rivers, and was finally appointed to the charge of the
Moreton Bay District. He named the Mary River after Lady Mary
Fitzroy, wife of the Governor, and as a compliment to him Sir Charles
caused the other large river in that district to be named the Burnett
in honour of him. Mr. Burnett died at his residence near Brisbane
on the 18th July, 1854, from premature decay of the system, which
was probably the manner of describing tuberculosis in those days.
A few days prior to his death he had the satisfaction of learning of
his election as a Fellow of the Royal Geographical Society of London.
Speaking of his death the "Moreton Bay Courier" says:—"By his
death society has lost a worthy member, and the Government an
active and zealous officer. There is some talk of a tablet to the
memory of the deceased. If the devotion of a life to the public
service gives any claim to such a tribute, it should not be left to
private friendship, but should emanate from the country at large."

The second survey of allotments at Toowoomba appears unmis-
takably to have been due to the representations made to the Surveyor-General by Mr. Assistant Surveyor E. O. Moriarty in his letter
of the 1st September, 1852, in which he pointed out the special
advantages of the "Swamp" as the site for a township. Though
Mr. Moriarty received instructions for the second survey of allotments at the "Swamp," the work did not fall to his lot, but was
performed by Mr. R. C. Bagot in April. 1853. Four sections of the
town included in the portion of the plan marked blue, and extending from a large morass, which occupied the portion of the town
where Campbell Street now intersects Ruthven Street, southward to
the corner of what is now known as Ruthven and Herries streets,

being bounded on the east and west sides by the swamps. These sections now form the main business centre of Toowoomba. The allotments were each about two acres in area, and in subdividing them three streets were laid out, Ruthven, Hume, and Margaret streets. These were the first streets named at the "Swamp." These allotments were submitted to sale at the Police Office. Drayton, on the 11th November, 1853, forty-seven being sold, no offer being received for five, and one forming part of the present Russell Street being reserved for the purpose of giving access to a waterhole situated in proximity to the spot where the Dominion Mill now stands. It would be wearisome in a paper of this kind to recall the names of the purchasers of the different allotments in the four sections comprised in the second survey, but as showing the increased value of land in Toowoomba since November, 1853, practically fifty years to a day, it will be interesting to compare the values of that day with the values of to-day. as estimated by the Municipal Valuator, which values may be taken as being about two-thirds of the owners' values. The first allotment sold on that occasion was the two-acre block on a portion of which the hall in which we now sit is erected. It realised £6 10s. per acre, and was purchased by Mr. A. Hodgson. Its present valuation is £20 per foot. The opposite corner of Ruthven and Herries streets, the latter then unnamed, was purchased by Mr. G. Partridge, father of Alderman Partridge, of this municipality, for £5 per acre, and the Council's valuation is now £28 per foot. The corner of Ruthven and Margaret streets, on which is built the Bank of New South Wales. was bought by Mr. C. Underwood for £10 per acre, and is now valued by the Council at £76 per foot. The opposite corner, on the west side of which is the warehouse of Billingtons Limited, was secured by Mr. W. Handcock at £11 per acre, and to-day the Council's value is £80 per foot. The corner on which the Australian Joint Stock Bank is built was purchased by Mr. J. P. Bell at £8 per acre, and is to-day valued by the Council at £80 per foot. On the opposite side, on which the Club Hotel now is built, Mr. W. Handcock bought two acres at £12 per acre, and the Council now estimates its value at £86 per foot. As already stated, the allotment forming a portion of Russell Street was reserved to give access to a waterhole, but the one south of it fell to the bid of Mr. T. Price at £9 per acre, and as an indication of the rise in values, some three or four years ago the balance of the Russell Street reserved allotment was sold at £107 per foot, with the improvements on it. Across the street Mr. C. Pottinger bought the allotment on which Messrs. Campbell Bros.' butcher's shop is located, at £9 5s. per acre, and its present valuation on the Council's books is £65 per foot. The Queensland National Bank corner was secured by Mr. T. Price at £12 per acre, and its present valuation is £58 per foot. No better idea of the extent to which property has increased in value during the last fifty years can be secured than by a careful study of these statistics of the present and the past. The next sale of land at the Swamp took place in June of 1854, when three blocks extending from Herries Street to Long Street on the west side of Ruthven Street were sold in two-acre allotments. at upset prices of £2 10s. and £4 per acre. The whole of the land was sold, but at very little beyond the upset values, the two highest prices being realised for the allotment at the corner of Ruthven and Herries streets, on the side of which this hall is built, which was purchased by Mr. J. McLelland at £7 5s. per acre, and the allotment at the south-east corner of Herries and Water streets, which fell to the bid of Mr. T. Price at £9 per acre.

We need not pursue land sales any further as the town at the Swamp was practically outlined, though it still rejoiced in the name of the "Swamp." The next feature of interest to us is that the settlement on this part of he Downs had assumed such proportions that Sir Charles Fitzroy, the Governor of New South Wales. thought it worth his while to visit the district when on a tour through the northern districts. He arrived at Drayton on the 29th March, 1854, the first Governor to visit the district, and was presented by the people with an address signed by Mr. afterwards Sir, Arthur Hodgson, at that time the leading man in the district, and by fifty-six others. He was also presented with an address from the school children, signed by each of them, and written by a pupil under ten years of age. At this early period of the settlement's history we have indisputable evidence that the young community had aspirations after a high civilisation, and was well disposed towards the education of the youth of the district. The new road from Ipswich, the head of navigation, to the Downs, was now approaching completion, and a " Government Gazette " notification in December of this year states that the new turn-pike gate on the road from Ipswich to Drayton shall be established as from January 1st, 1855. The remains of this old turn-pike, which was veritably a gate to the richness of the South and West, are still to be observed. The " Swamp " continued to participate in all the progress which was being made, as the two following extracts from the " Moreton Bay Courier " will show. Its Drayton correspondent, writing on September 22nd, 1854 : " The new township, or, as it is called, the Swamp, is rapidly assuming an attractive appearance. It bids fair to outdo the old township. The situation is much better adapted for a town, and ere long we doubt not but that it will become the Goulburn of the northern districts. It is much to be regretted that the Government did not at first make the township of Drayton higher up the Swamp. It will sooner or later be the principal place of business." These were prophetic words, for not only is it the principal place of business, but it has outrivalled Goulburn.

Writing in May of 1856, the same correspondent says:—" The two settlements are going ahead rapidly. In the course of two or three years Ipswich will be nothing to them. At the Swamp in particular houses are erecting week after week. There is a great outcry for land there. One gentleman residing at the "Swamp" is selling portions of his estate as high as £100 per acre. Respecting the old town of Drayton, or West Drayton, as it will probably be called, it is not dying away as some people thought." From this passage we may gather that a choice of a name is beginning to agitate the minds of the people of the "Swamp," from which no doubt may also be dated the commencement of the rivalry between the two places which for a period of six or seven years disturbed the harmony of the settlements.

So far I have to acknowledge my indebtedness to the Survey Office, and the files of the "Moreton Bay Courier" for the information I have been able to place before you. Unfortunately the files of the "Moreton Bay Courier" are missing from 1st January, 1857, to 1st July, 1858. a period of almost absorbing interest, since it is within that period that the name Toowoomba was given to the "Swamp," by whom, and under what circumstances, must, I think, remain in doubt and be for ever legendary. It is generally accepted that Toowoomba is an aboriginal word, but various meanings are assigned to it By some it is declared to mean "the meeting of the waters." As early as 1860, in discussing the incorporation of the town, Mr. J. C. White, by implication rather than by direct statement, declared that the meaning of the word was "great in the future," but Mr. A. Meston, an accepted authority on aboriginal nomenclature, informs me that there can be no possible doubt that the name is derived from "choowoom," the name of a small melon about the size of a duck's egg. which once grew prolifically within the district. The suffix "ba" means the place, or "there"; hence Choowoomba means the place where the "choowoom" grows. There is still another origin assigned to the name. Just as the name "Yankee" is a North American Indian corruption of the French attempt to pronounce the word "English," so it is asserted that the word Toowoomba is a corruption of a corruption. It is held that the best efforts of the aboriginals to pronounce the word "swamp" could only produce "Tchwampa." which by easy transitions became "Twamba," and finally "Toowoomba." This latter origin may after all be the true one, though Mr. Meston is most emphatic as to the correctness of the meaning he assigns, and declares he was personally acquainted with aboriginals who described the "choowoom," and the place where it grew to him. But whatever may have been the origin of the name, it is certain that when we once again get on the solid ground of authentic history the "Swamp" has become Toowoomba.

On the 10th June, 1858, the "Darling Downs Gazette," now the property of Mr. S. C. W. Robinson and myself, was first published in Drayton by Mr. Arthur Sidney Lyon, who previously had called into existence the "Moreton Bay Courier" in Brisbane, and the "North Australian" in Ipswich, and the growth of the town in commercial and social importance is noted from week to week in its files. In the very first issue we note that the Rev. Dr. Nelson, father of the President of the Royal Geographical Society, Sir H. M. Nelson, whom we have with us to-day, solicits subscriptions for a new "Church of Scotland," which it is proposed to build in Toowoomba. He required about £180, and asked that the subscriptions might be sent to Ipswich, his then headquarters, or to the local secretary, the late Hon. W. H. Groom, who from that time forward was identified with almost every social movement in the district up to the time of his death two years ago. In a leading article in the "Gazette" on the 20th June, 1858, the fact that there were no public houses in Toowoomba is deplored, and Drayton is urged to attract people to that township or she will be left behind in the race for supremacy. During the next week or two land changed hands at from £60 to £130 per acre, the latter being given for land situated near the reservoir, close to the bridge in Margaret Street East. About this time the late Hon. Jas. Taylor seems to have become a leading figure in the social life of the community, invariably presiding on the bench at Drayton, and in other ways promoting the commercial and social interests of the inhabitants. Among other things it may be noted that at this time he introduced the first steam saw-milling plant capable of turning out at that period the astonishingly large quantity of 1,000 feet per day. The incensed sawyers on the Range threatened to punch holes in the boiler. The stigma of no hotel accommodation was removed in July, 1858, for Captain Witham re-opened the "Queen's Arms" Hotel, on the site of the present Club Hotel, Mr. F. Mole the present Royal Hotel, and Mr. John Dare the Sovereign Hotel, which stood near the site of Mr. W. Williamson's residence in Ruthven Street South. In other ways the town is showing signs of progress, for a School of Arts became an accomplished fact on the 19th August of the same year. Mr. Jas. Taylor was elected President, Mr. D. W. Campbell Secretary, and Messrs. W. H. Groom, M. Boulton, J. Wilson, and J. Berkman the provisional committee. This was the first instance of the ballot being used on this part of the Downs. August 28th of this year is important in the annals of Toowoomba, since on that date a public meeting was held at the Royal Hotel, with Mr. Jas. Taylor in the chair, for the purpose of protesting against the annexation of Too-woomba to Drayton. A memorial was addressed to the Secretary of Public Lands and Works on the subject, pointing out the injustice which would be done to Toowoomba, which contained a population of nearly one thousand, of whom about two hundred were freeholders, owning land in the township valued between ten and twenty thousand pounds sterling. St. Luke's School for girls was opened on October 14th of the same year, and was followed by one for the boys a few weeks later. In November, Mr. A. Hodgson, from his place in the House, asked why Toowoomba had not been proclaimed a township, and was informed that the reason was the boundaries had not yet been determined. In May, 1859, extreme dissatisfaction was expressed at Mr. Burrowes, the Land Commissioner, having fixed the boundaries of Toowoomba between the two swamps, cutting out the whole of the present West Ward and portion of the South. A correspondent to the "Gazette" declares that Mr. Burrowes had attended a dinner in Drayton where the proposed boundaries were discussed, and that the discussion influenced him. On the 12th May a public meeting was held with Mr. Jas. Taylor in the chair, and it was resolved to memorialise the Secretary for Lands and Public Works, the Hon. John Robertson, on the need to include in Toowoomba the first survey of Toowoomba, and also the land on the east side of the East Swamp to the summit of the range. In June the present Racecourse Reserve was granted for the purpose of a recreation ground for the people of Drayton and Toowoomba. Owing to there being no suitable building at Drayton, the committee of the Drayton Benevolent Society, Messrs. Jas. Taylor, John Watts, W. Armstrong. M.D., and the Rev. B. Glennie, determined to establish the Home in Toowoomba. This was done, and in time the Drayton Benevolent Society became the Toowoomba Hospital, whose foundation may therefore be said to date from 1859. A correspondent of the "Gazette," writing on August 25th of this year, estimates the value of landed property in the township at £18,000, and suggests the imposition of a tax of one shilling in the pound in order to raise funds for a proper water supply. Fifty years have not removed the water supply grievance, but the bare suggestion of a shilling in the pound tax for the purpose of securing a sufficient supply of water would cause the taxpayers of to-day to break out in a cold perspiration. At the end of twelve months the attendance of pupils at the St. Luke's schools was found to be sixty-seven. As separation was practically an accomplished fact, many schemes were suggested for the division of Queensland into electorates. One such scheme was outlined by the late Hon. W. H. Groom in the columns of the "Gazette." suggesting one representative for Drayton, with a population of 400, and one for Toowoomba, with a population of 1,000. These statistics prove that the early prophecies had come true. Drayton was far outdistanced in the race by the younger township of Toowoomba.

The question of the proclamation of Toowoomba as a town is again brought up by a " Gazette" correspondent, under date 3rd January, 1860, when he asks for information on the subject, and is informed that as separation has now taken place the proceedings to secure that object will need to be commenced *de novo*. The growing jealousy between Drayton and Toowoomba found vent at a public meeting held in the latter township on March 12th, 1860, for the purpose of making arrangements for the reception of the new Governor. Sir Geo. Bowen. A suggestion that both townships should combine was negatived by the Toowoomba people, who were determined to stand alone. Next night a counter meeting was held in Drayton at the Royal Bull's Head, with Dr. Armstrong in the chair, and the narrow mindedness of the Toowoomba people was severely commented upon by the chairman. Drayton also decided to have its reception. On the 12th inst. the Circuit Court sat for the first time in Toowoomba, being previously conducted in Drayton. Judge Lutwyche presided.

On the 29th March, His Excellency Sir G. F. Bowen visited Toowoomba on his way from Warwick and Drayton. He was met on the road by two hundred horsemen and conducted to Toowoomba. A triumphal arch was erected in front of Dare's Hotel, where a brass band was also stationed on the verandah, and played " God Save the Queen," as His Excellency passed on to Mole's Hotel, where apartments had been provided for him. There he was presented with an address by Mr. J. C. White, and in replying to it His Excellency urged Drayton and Toowoomba to unite under the new name of " Victoria." In the evening he was entertained at a dinner given in his honour at Witham's Hotel. It is thus seen that the honours of the reception were equally divided among the three inn-keepers, which then, as in small communities of to-day, no doubt tended to preserve harmony in the district. Meetings at Drayton and Toowoomba urging the establishment of municipalities now became very frequent. On the 10th April a meeting was held in Drayton, and a deputation was appointed to a meeting to be held in Toowoomba on the 13th to see if a basis of union could be agreed upon. The meeting was held, and the deputationists having expressed their views, Mr. W. H. Groom moved: " That this meeting, having heard the reasons assigned by the Drayton deputation for seeking the co-operation of the Toowoomba people in the formation of a joint municipality, courteously declines the proposed amalgamation, and desires to record its opinion that as the rapid progress Toowoomba has made within the last four years, and its present healthy and flourishing condition, is entirely owing to the industry, untiring perseverance, and indomitable courage of the Toowoombians themselves, it is expedient and highly necessary they should take the constitutional course to have their locality proclaimed a munipality,

free and distinct from any other town." This was seconded by Mr.
Annand, and carried with a considerable majority.

The result of this meeting was considerable bitterness between
the two townships, and some newspaper correspondence. But while
Toowoomba and Drayton are fighting for incorporation, the first
political battle in Queensland is being fought. The candidates for
Drayton and Toowoomba were Mr. John Watts, a brother-in-law of
our President, the Right Hon. Sir H. M. Nelson, and Mr. T. B.
Stephens, father of the present senior member for South Brisbane.
The election took place on 2nd May, 1860, and resulted as follows :—
Watts, 119; Stephens, 37; majority for Watts, 82. On the 17th
May about 120 persons met in the Argyle Rooms to urge the incorporation of the town. A suggestion that a memorial be presented
to the Governor, asking for an incorporation of the two townships.
under the name of " Queenstown," was negatived, and on the motion
of Mr. J. C. White, seconded by Mr. Boulton, it was resolved to
ask for the incorporation of Toowoomba, either with or without
Drayton, as the Governor thought fit. On June 23rd, a petition
for incorporation bearing over a hundred signatures was sent to Sir
Geo. Bowen, through Mr. J. Watts, M.L.A., and in response to his
request Toowoomba was proclaimed a corporate town on the 21st
July, 1860.

Several months were spent in making the preliminary arrangements before a municipal election could be held. The election finally
eventuated on the 4th January, 1861, when the following gentlemen
were returned as the first Municipal Council :—W. H. Groom, 51;
M. M'Carty, 40: Jas. Berkman, 35; W. Shuttlewood, 31; M. Boulton, 30; John Robertson, 26; W. Annand, 25; Jas. Peardon, 24;
and Patrick Ryan, 23. The same evening a meeting of the newly-
elected Council was held, and Mr. W. H. Groom was chosen to fill
the position of the first Mayor of the municipality. Of this first
Council, Mr. P. Ryan is still alive, residing in James Street, and I
believe Mr. Peardon is also alive. The whole of the others have
passed to their rest, having well done their part in laying the foun-
dations of the municipality whose history from that time has been one
of uninterrupted progress.

The election of the first Municipal Council marks the closing of
the early history of Toowoomba. From that time it enters upon a
new era. My work is completed with the first period of the township's existence and struggles for a more fully developed commercial
and social life. If the records of a bygone period which I have been
able to dig up out of a buried past have proved of interest to those
who are present, and if they are likely to be of value to the Royal
Geographical Society of Queensland, I shall feel pleased that I have
been able to contribute to your pleasure, and to have assisted in the
work of the Society.

MARITIME BOUNDARY OF QUEENSLAND.*

By the Hon. JOHN DOUGLAS, C.M G., F.R.G.S.

(Hon. Member Royal Geographical Society of Australasia, Queensland.)

I am honoured by thus having audience of the Royal Geographical Society of Queensland, and I beg to crave the attention of members for a brief space while I expound my theme on a matter of some general geographical interest, and one of special local significance to those of us who are connected, as I am, with the islands of Torres Straits, and the somewhat important little dependency of Thursday Island and Port Kennedy.

There is a tradition that a commission was sent out to Sir John Young, authorising him to extend the boundary of New South Wales to the 10th parallel of south latitude. I cannot ascertain whether it was ever acted on. Let me, however, relate how it was that the islands of Torres Straits came to be annexed.

In 1876-7 certain adventurous spirits connected with the pearl-shelling industry had pushed out beyond the recognised bounds of our jurisdiction, and it was found that there was no legal authority which could be brought to bear upon them. It became necessary, therefore, to extend the boundaries of Queensland, and after a good deal of correspondence this was finally accomplished by the passing of an Act of the Queensland Parliament in 1879, which had been duly authorised by letters patent under the Great Seal.

Thus it was that "certain islands in Torres Straits and lying between the continent of Australia and island of New Guinea, that is to say, all islands included within a line drawn from Sandy Cape northward to the south-eastern limit of the Great Barrier Reefs, thence following the line of the great Barrier Reefs to their north-eastern extremity, near the latitude of $9\frac{1}{2}$ deg., thence in a north-westerly direction, embracing East Anchor and Bramble Cay, thence from Bramble Cay in a line west by south (true), embracing Warrior Reef, Saibai, and Tuan Island, thence diverging in a north-westerly direction, so as to embrace the group known as the Talbot Islands, thence to and embracing the Deliverance Islands, and onwards in a west by south direction to the meridian of 138 deg. of east longitude."

That then is the present boundary of Queensland. When it was thus defined it was considered desirable to annex everything up to the shores of New Guinea. The annexation of British New Guinea did not take place for some nine years after this, but it then soon became

---

* Read before the Royal Geographical Society of Australasia, December 22, 1903.

apparent that some modification of the boundary in Torres Straits was necessary. This became the subject of correspondence between Sir William M'Gregor, the Colonial Office, and the Government of Queensland. . . In 1892 Sir Samuel Griffith, then being in office visited Torres Straits on purpose to satisfy himself on the merits of the case, and I have no doubt that it would then soon have been settled, but unfortunately for this particular matter then in hand, Sir Samuel became Chief Justice, and nothing more was done until the correspondence was again revived, and at last various propositions were made and rejected. In May, 1898, an Order-in-Council altering the boundary, was passed, and such alteration was to take effect upon the passing of an Act of Parliament by Queensland endorsing it. The Act was duly drafted, printed, and prepared for the approval of Parliament, but unfortunately again, it was never brought in, and nothing more was done. I shall now proceed to describe to you what the alteration was which it was thus proposed to effect.

Starting from a point three miles south-east of Bramble Cay, on the existing boundary line, it was designed to pass midway between Pearce Cay and Dalrymple Island, then by the centre of Moon Pass in the Warrior Reef, thence by a line passing three miles to the south of Turnagain and Deliverance Islands, westerly, thence west by south to the meridian of the 138th degree of east longitude. But, as I have said, this was never authorised. Soon after the Commonwealth came into existence, and with it the capacity of Queensland to deal solely with the matter, passed to the Commonwealth. Now, we know that the Commonwealth Parliament is about to legislate for British New Guinea, or for Papua, as it is to be called, and that is why I am anxious to draw attention to the maritime boundary of Queensland as affecting the maritime boundary of Papua, in order that it may be clearly understood.

In the first place, allow me to say that, in my opinion, the boundary, as defined by the Order-in-Council of 1898, ought to be accepted as a fair and reasonable solution of the question. It was arrived at after an exhaustive correspondence between the parties concerned, and would, I feel sure, be gladly accepted by the Papuan Government authorities as a just solution of their claims, for they have undoubted claims to a rectification of the existing boundary. So far as regards the Government of Queensland, it ought to be a relief to them to be able to hand over to the Papuan Government islands which they are not able satisfactorily to govern from Thursday Island. Moreover, the Papuan Government, by its special ordinances, made applicable to native requirements, is much more capable of administering justice and maintaining order than we are. I have done the best I can to administer justice and maintain order in a patriarchal kind of way through the head men, or mamooses, as they are called, of the different

D—ROYAL GEO. SOCIETY.

islands, and the people generally carry out my wishes, but something more than this is now required. It is difficult, nay almost impossible, to apply our Queensland laws to such islands as Saibai, Dowan, and Boigo. To the magistrate at Daru, with his native ordinances, and his proximity to these islands, it is another matter altogether. The people inhabiting these islands are Papuans. They are most amenable to order. They have improved immensely. When I first knew them they were literally naked savages. Now they are among the most intelligent and enterprising of our islanders. But, like most natives, they are easily led astray. Unprincipled men, both white and coloured, give or sell them drink, and through Saibai a good deal of liquor has been supplied to the natives of New Guinea. Indeed, so frequently has this been lately done that the authorities at Daru have prohibited our Saibai natives from landing on the shores of New Guinea. I have done the best I can to stop this nefarious traffic in liquor, and I am happy to say that I have secured two convictions; but this is not such an easy matter, for the proceedings have to be conducted in accordance with the laws of the State before the court at Thursday Island, which is eighty miles from Saibai. In the last case five witnesses had to be brought in and taken out again in order to secure the necessary evidence. Such cases would, I can assure you, be much more easily and effectually disposed of at Daru, the western headquarters of administration in British New Guinea. That is one very good reason why I should like to see Saibai under the jurisdiction at Daru. There are many other reasons, but geographically—and you, gentlemen, are specially interested in the question from that point of view—it does seem ridiculous that a large island like Saibai, being almost within gunshot of New Guinea, should still belong to Queensland. Nor must it be forgotten that as Government Resident at Thursday Island I have now no steamer in which I can visit these Islands. This year, it is true, I have visited the coast of New Guinea four times in order to investigate matters of this kind; but it has always been in a small sailing vessel, and this does not further prompt action. What I have said of Saibai holds good of Dowan (Tuan) and of Boigo. They are both visited and occupied by Papuans, and they are both tarred with the same brush so far as the distribution of liquor is concerned. I am sorry to say it, for the Papuan, as a rule, has no great longing for our liquors, unless he is educated in that direction by the white man. He is satisfied with the mild excitements of the betel nut until he reaches a higher exaltation under the influence of our liquor essences. Of course you all know that under our laws persons are prohibited from supplying liquor to aboriginal natives, or to South Sea Islanders, and at Thursday Island we are sometimes held up as examples of how a good law may be violated with the most impunity. A distinguished visitor, a senator from the

South, for instance, remarked the other day that he saw aboriginal natives served at the bars of public-houses with the police looking calmly on. This, I admit is perfectly true. There appears to be great apathy on their part. When challenged, however, with negligence of duty, they say that they arrest offenders who exceed, and that they prefer the open violation of the law as practised to the illicit sale of bottles and cases of grog through intermediate persons. They also say that it is almost impossible to secure a conviction against a publican who sells to an aboriginal across the bar, for the law requires proof that the liquor so sold contains or contained so much per cent. of alcohol. How are they to prove that, they say, when the alcohol is absorbed into the stomach of the participant? I fancy myself that a way out of that difficulty might be found. Still, the fact remains that no complaints are lodged, and convictions are rarely obtained. To revert, however, once more to the theme of my paper, which I do not wish to make tedious, there are manifest advantages connected with the proposed rectifinition. No one can question its geographical justification. It will fairly meet the claims of the Papuan Government, and it will in no way prejudice the territorial rights of this State. The trade of that portion of New Guinea, such as it is, gravitates to Thursday Island, and will continue to do so. It gives reasonable scope to the natives of Papua for the prosecution of their pearl-shelling industry, to which they are by no means indifferent, and it will enable the Papuan Government to control and repress altogether, I hope, this nefarious dealing in liquor, which is calculated to do so much harm if it is allowed to go on.

Before I close this paper I must honestly tell you that before the desired object can be attained considerable difficulties stand in the way. The rectifications could easily have been effected in 1892, after Sir Samuel's exploration, or, indeed, in 1898, when the Order-in-Council authorising it was passed; but now there is rather a formidable lion in the path. The 123rd clause of the Commonwealth Constitution provides that " the Parliament of the Commonwealth may, with the consent of the Parliament of the State, and the approval of the electors of the State voting upon the question, increase, diminish, otherwise alter the limits of the State, on such terms and conditions as may be agreed on, and may, with the like consent, make provision respecting the effect and operation of any increase, diminution, or alteration of territory in relation to any State affected." As I have said, this is rather a formidable lion; but it can be tackled and required to retreat in this particular case if we can show, as I think we can, that he stands in the way of what would be a decided improvement.

Sir S. W. Griffith, in proposing a hearty vote of thanks to Mr. Douglas, said very few persons even in Queensland knew how very interesting these parts were. They were attracting attention from scientific people in Europe, and there was an expedition on its way now to study natural history in that part of Australian waters, which had peculiarities not found anywhere else.   With regard to the boundary, when it was fixed in 1878, it was not unreasonable for Queensland to require to get all she could. She could not get New Guinea, but managed to get as near as possible.   We followed round as close as we could get between the islands, and the coast of New Guinea· taking in practically everything.   At that time all these parts were equally unknown, and unsettled ; but later, when New Guinea had what was after all a civilised Government, and in some respects a highly organised Government, considering the nature of the people it had to deal with, it became extremely absurd that some of the islands should be governed by Queensland because, as Mr. Douglas had pointed out, Queensland laws were quite inapplicable, whereas New Guinea laws were perfectly applicable.   That impressed itself so strongly on his (Sir S. W. Griffith's) mind that in order to remove the anomaly, he took the opportunity of going up there in the steamer Lucinda.   Mr. Douglas was with him, and the trip was extremely interesting. It was hardly necessary to go up to see how absurd the arrangement was ; but up there it appeared much more absurd.   To illustrate this, he mentioned that when Sir William MacGregor defeated an invading tribe some of them escaped to the islands, where, being in Queensland territory, he could not interfere with them.   Few concerned in the Government of the Commonwealth, and few in Queensland, knew anything of the matter.   The cash value of the whole territory involved was not more than £100 or £200 ; but it was a serious matter that involved the welfare of a great number of very decent people.   The first thing was to get the people to understand the facts ; when they did, there would not be two opinions as to the correct thing to do.   The next thing was, What was to be done ?   The Parliament of Queensland must consent to the alteration of the boundaries of the State of Queensland, by giving up these island to New Guinea.   In the next place the Parliament of the Commonwealth must consent, and then the electors of Queensland must consent when the matter was submitted to them.   He suggested that at the next general elections ballot papers on this question should be submitted to the people, and this could be done at little cost.

Sir Hugh Nelson : About one in 1000 would vote.

Sir S. W. Griffith said if only five voted and three were in favour it would be sufficient.   If he had an opportunity of communicating with any one concerned in taking the necessary steps it would give him the greatest pleasure.   (Applause.)

Sir A. C. Gregory seconded the motion, and said it was important to include the whole of the islands with Queensland at the time ; but the moment New Guinea had a separate Government the conditions changed.

The motion was carried with acclamation.

NEW ZEALAND:

Its Geographical and Meteorological Conditions Considered in their Bearing on Field Industries.*

By GEORGE WOOLNOUGH, M.A.

Mr. President, Ladies, and Gentlemen,—I must premise that recently I went to New Zealand on holiday. At the same time I resolved to look around for forces at work, producing present real or apparent prosperity in that country. It may assist you in judging the value of my paper, if I indicate on a map the routes over which I passed. On landing at Wellington I went to the Lower Hutt to see the beautiful botanical gardens which are there. Arriving at Port Lyttelton, I entrained for Timaru, crossing the famous Canterbury Plains. From Dunedin, I went by railway, due south, to Balclutha; thence west to Lumsden; then northwards to Kingston. Lake Whakatipu, 20 miles to Queenstown, and 30 more to Glenorchy, is travelled by what is playfully called a pleasure steamer. Returning to Wellington, I took train for New Plymouth, thus crossing the south-west side of the Northern Island. From New Plymouth, by steamer, to Auckland. There I took train for Rotorua, running, for the distance, down almost the centre of the Northern Island. From Auckland I went by steamer along the eastern coast to Gisborne and Napier. At the last-named place I entrained again, for Wellington, running over the south-east part of the island. It thus may be seen that I passed over a great deal of country, and along many miles of coast, and that I had opportunity for seeing what other travellers see, under similar circumstances. Also, during my visit I saw and conversed with all sorts of persons likely to give me information. Specially I visited the Roslyn wool factory at Dunedin, and the Gear meatworks at Wellington. In both cases the proprietors and managers were most obliging, permitting me to see all that there was to be seen, and fully answering all questions. I came to the conclusion that the forces there at work for good are found (a) in the great natural resources of the country; (b) in the character of the people themselves; (c) in some of the conditions of their communal life; and (d) largely in the geographical and meteorological conditions of the country in their bearing on field industries.

Speaking before your Society, I confine myself to the last of these four things; though I should much like to speak on all of the others, especially on the second of them. Indeed, for the purposes

---

* Read before the Royal Geographical Society of Australasia, Q , May 28, 1904.

of my paper it seems necessary to say that I looked for a New
Zealand type; but did not see one anywhere save at Dunedin. There
I saw boys and girls, young men and maidens, typical of parentage
and climate. The absence of type is a little perplexing, for the
population of New Zealand is so largely native born. The percentages
are: Native born, 66; Australian, 4; Great Britain and Ireland. 26;
divided as follows—England, 14.5; Scotland, 6.20; Ireland. 5.64;
and Wales, 0.22. Nevertheless, one was impressed by the fact that
he was in a community of workers.

Perhaps, without visiting New Zealand, wholly by studying maps
and returns, one might learn all of the main facts now to be dealt
with by me; but, from experience, I am able to say that on a visit
one is more deeply impressed than otherwise he could be. I first call
your attention to the

"GEOGRAPHICAL SITUATION"

of the islands of New Zealand. A visitor, at first, is impressed chiefly
by the painful fact that he must make a voyage of about 1,200 miles
from the nearest part of the mainland of Australia before he can set
foot in New Zealand. Sometimes that voyage makes the traveller
wish that New Zealand were either so far off that he would not be
tempted to pay a visit there; or so near that his misery at sea would
be very brief. But even a visitor has to look at his map to see
exactly the outline of New Zealand, and also its many island portions.
The group used to be smaller; but in April, 1842, by royal letters
patent, and again by the Imperial Act 26 and 27 Vict., c. 23 (1863),
the boundaries of the country were altered, and made to extend
from 33 degrees to 53 degrees of south latitude; and from 162 degrees
of east longitude to 173 degrees of west longitude. By proclamation
afterwards, and also quite recently, many islands have been added,
so that the entire territory is made up of eleven groups of islands,
comprising 104,751 square miles, in which are islands not available
for settlement, having an area of 498 square miles. Here at once is a
group of objects strong and silent, yet ever at work, aiding to produce
those meteorological results called atmospheric pressure, temperature,
and humidity, recognised by us as wind or calm, heat or cold, cloud
or sunshine. I do not know if I am right but it appears to me that
there is not another country in the world so admirably situated for
supplying meteorological data from which approximately the most
reliable forecasts of weather may be made. Only a thoroughly
scientific treatment of the subject would suffice for safety and utility;
and I do not pretend to have the skill, certainly I have not the
time, for the work. But in passing the following observations may
be made. The average of highest temperatures at eight principal
stations was 83.32 degrees, the highest of them being 90.5 degrees,
the lowest of them being 72 degrees; this was at Chatham Islands.

The average of the lowest temperatures was nearly 30 degrees; the highest of them was 38 degrees—namely, at Auckland; and the lowest was 25.9 degrees nearly 6 degrees of cold; this was at Christchurch. The average number of wet days was 184. The greatest number was 245, at New Plymouth; the smallest number, 120, was at Rotorua. The total rainfall for the year in the eight districts was: Auckland, 38.28 inches; Rotorua, 48.72; New Plymouth, 52.04; Wellington, 38.75; Hokitika, 96.07; Lincoln College, Canterbury, 24.49; Dunedin, 53.54; Chatham Islands, 39.62. The average of all these is nearly 49 inches. This is only a statement of the facts; it is not in any sense an analysis of them; nor does the statistician whose figures I have summarised give any analysis of his own data. He does supply a really remarkable table compiled from information published in the statistical abstract for the colonial possessions of the United Kingdom; but he leaves his readers to do their own analytic work.

In view of all the above, I feel no hesitation when saying that with climatic conditions, such as prevail here, land in New Zealand could not yield such abundant crops as are said to be garnered there. Approximately the following statement will show our rainfall for last year. At nine stations in the north-east the average fall was 75.3 inches. In the north-west the average fall at eight stations was 31.09 inches. In the central district at nine stations the average fall was 18.03 inches. In the south-eastern part of the southern district, at 23 stations, the average fall was 7.06 inches; and in the south-western part of the same district the average fall was 11.16 inches. Those totals give an average fall of 28.6 for the whole of Queensland. And that was in a comparatively wet year. In connection with this, consider our higher temperature and drier atmosphere; and then on comparison it may more fully be seen how favourable are climatic conditions to field industries in New Zealand.

The island character of New Zealand, with its 4,500 miles of coastline, for its three main islands, has much to do with its internal formation and its soil. The North Island, covering about 45,000 square miles, has one volcanic mountain and several high hills, which cover at least one-tenth of the area. It is what we call " unavailable " country. There are large areas of comparatively level country; some small ones, and some valleys, most of them having a light soil; but much of it is heavily timbered; and some of it is swamp. The agricultural area, thus made up, is set down at 13,000,000 acres; the purely pastoral area is set down at 14,200,000 acres. A remarkable feature of this must be pointed out. It is said to be especially suited for English grasses. Everyone who has had experience in English grasses, in a well-watered district in Australia, knows that by their use pastoral areas are made to carry three times as many stock as can

be carried on them if only natural grasses are there.   The Middle
Island, having an area of about 59,000 square miles, also is moun-
tainous and hilly.   The area of level or undulating land in the Middle
Island available for agriculture is estimated at about 15,000,000
acres.   About 13,000,000 are suitable for pastoral purposes only, or
may become so when cleared of forest and sown with grass-seed.   The
proportions of agricultural and pastoral land, in the two islands, thus
are seen to be as 28,000,000 acres to 27,000,000 acres.   The traveller
is sure to observe. in both islands, very large areas of very poor land—
rabbit country, goat country.   There are, in all, at least 10,000,000
acres of such land.   In the extreme south. climate is not so favourable to farming.   Sometimes an unripened crop will remain in the
field all winter.   Speaking now of

FIELD PRODUCTS.

I point out that objects which give greatest promise are most largely
cultivated, climate and soil being duly considered.   They are ordinary
cereals, tubers, fruits, and cattle.   So much has been said in regard
to the first of these that I shall give a few very exact details.   One
day at Timaru, a cabman informed me that once upon a time land
in New Zealand yielded 100 bushels of dressed wheat per acre.   On
my expressing a doubt, he admitted that perhaps he should have
said oats.   Some time afterwards a clergyman remarked to me that
once upon a time land in New Zealand yielded 100 bushels of dressed
wheat to the acre.   I suggested oats. but the clergyman, as was
proper, held his ground.   Since my return to Brisbane I have encountered a man who assured me that once upon a time land in New
Zealand yielded 100 bushels of dressed wheat per acre.   Again I
suggested oats, but he lost his temper, and assured me that his statement was correct, for he was living in New Zealand at the time.
Both the cabman and the clergyman might have used the same fact
in support of the statement.   Had they and all other persons similarly situated done likewise, it is hard to see how any man could
longer harbour unbelief.   But it is a fact, on the authority of the
last New Zealand official yearbook. that the average yield of wheat
for the past 13 years was 26 bushels per acre.   The yield for the year
1902 was the highest for the period given ; it gave an average of
33.98 bushels per acre.   Taranaki gave the highest average—namely,
40 bushels per acre.   The yield of wheat in Queensland last year was,
I believe, set down at an average of less than 20 bushels per acre.
The yield of other cereals in New Zealand is given in authorised
returns: and, as may be expected, they tally fairly well with the
wheat returns.   A similar remark may be made concerning tubers.
A British-born man or woman is delighted on seeing so many sorts
of old country fruits.   When I saw all these things. the one word
that incessantly ran through the mind was " climate." It accounted

for the extra beautiful dahlia blooms, the tall hollyhook, the daisy, and also for the sturdy form of the English dock and the Scotch thistle. Equally the climate accounts for the superb cattle, sheep, and horses of the country. Nowhere in Australia can be seen such horses as the Clydesdales of Dunedin. Scarcely did I anywhere see a poor-conditioned horse. Summer is the best season at which to see them, I know; but there they were, massive, sleek, strong, docile. I did not learn that there were any unions among them; and yet, if anywhere the horse is a happy animal, that place is New Zealand. Some parts of the country are cold enough severely to punish cattle, and occasionally sheep are lost in the snow. In the North Island may be seen the methods used to produce the incomparable crossbred mutton, of which New Zealand has sent so much to British markets. In its commercial aspects this is a very large subject; I mention it now only that I may point out once more the influence of climate. At the Gear meatworks, at Wellington, I saw about 3,000 mutton and lamb carcases. They looked as if the living animals must have been bred and fattened under the most genial circumstances; as if they had not suffered a day's thirst on the road to the works; they were models of form and condition. In the middle of January, the temperature in the cooling-room stood at 50 degrees Fahr. Once more the word "climate" came into mind.

From the above conditions, two remarkable, mutually reciprocal results take place. I first speak of the equable

DISTRIBUTION OF POPULATION.

In Victoria 41 per cent. of the people live in Melbourne. In New South Wales, Sydney claims 36 per cent. of the population; whereas Auckland, the metropolis of New Zealand, has only a little more than 8 per cent. of the people; Wellington, the capital, has a little more than 6 per cent.; Christchurch, the Boston of the country, has a little more than 7 per cent.; and Dunedin, the new Edinburgh, has about 6.4 per cent. of the entire white population. It is esti- mated that not more than 30 per cent. of the people live in towns having a population of more than 10,000 souls. Beside boroughs, there are 35 town districts, portions of counties in which they are situated, in only one of which districts does the population exceed 1,000 inhabitants. Then also there are 683 places in the nature of townships, villages, or centres of population. This important fact arrests the attention of the traveller. He observes that the people are on the land, because that is where are to be carried out so many of the industries by which we live. If we think of it we must feel sure that the simplest if the hardest industries, that of the field, always will attract the strong, comparatively unskilled, and unam- bitious youth of the community. At the same time they are attracted by the healthy, domestic, and humane character of field and homestead life. Manufacturing has not yet set up a very powerful counter attraction; and, as to factory life, if more money is earned, and if workers appear to have more freedom, they certainly have not either the health or the comfort of even yeoman farming life. These facts were noted by Dr. Victor S. C.ark, who recently visited New Zealand to report on labour conditions there, by direction of the United States Government. He said "the population is rather evenly distributed in four main groups, around as many urban centres; and in this respect the colony is quite different from its Australian neighbours, each with its preponderating metropolis." The New Zealand people themselves are rather proud of this fact. Officially they say, "While New South Wales and Victoria present what is termed by the statistician of the former State ' the disquieting spectacle of capital towns growing with wonderful rapidity, and embracing in their limits one-third of the population of the territory of which they are the centre,' New Zealand is saved from this by the configuration of the country." We need not dispute over the cause here assigned for the aforesaid distribution; but I stand by my statement. The configuration of the country in itself could not account for the whole of the result, for if the interior of the country did not contain fertile land, watered by abundant rains, and warmed by genial sunshine, island formed as the country is, there would not be more persons distributed over it than may be found in a corresponding area of our never-never country.

The other result intended by me is seen in the equable

DISTRIBUTION OF PROSPERITY.

A discussion of this great economic subject would lie outside the line which encloses your Society. But I mention it because in one respect it is germane to my theme. At least it may be brought in under an expression used in the heading of my paper; to wit, "the apparent" prosperity of New Zealand.

Where persons live in a state of nature, camping in the open, living on natural products, uncooked, there all alike are rich and all alike are poor. At the moment when accumulation begins, differences as between rich and poor develop. As accumulation augments, the differences become greater; till we have millionaires, if not paupers The great economic problem of the day is so to work that accumulation shall not be checked; and so to govern that it shall not be too unequally distributed. New Zealand, above any country, ancient or modern, known to us, has attempted, whilst allowing competition, to reduce this proposition to practical form. She boasts that to a large extent she has succeeded; and she has. It is so much in evidence that no observing person can visit that country without seeing it. But whoever has seen it, and also a striking example of a converse character, must be tempted to consider which, after all, is the better of the two. Again I quote from Dr. Victor S. Clark. In his report to his Government, published in a bulletin of the "Bureau of Labour," he says, after looking at New Zealand as to the distribution of prosperity there, "it is not in a dead level of material comfort that the real prosperity of a nation consists. That was provided by the Incas of Peru. But it is in the constant incentive to individual enterprise, in untrammelled ambition, in the consciousness of the call to labour on the part of every member of the community. The ' strenuous life ' is already a well worn term in our country, but it contains the secret of living for the present generation of Americans. We cannot but instinctively recoil from the thought of a State protectorate over our individual activities. The nation is largely composed of people whose ancestors, or who themselves, have devoted energy and sacrifice to getting away from that very thing. Labouring men say that the Arbitration Act in New Zealand has killed the ' fighting spirit ' of the unions. That is possibly a social gain ; but what American employer even does not feel a secret dislike of the situation it implies? In other words, our habits of thought and temperamental sympathies are not in accord with those dominant in New Zealand. The ways of the latter country may be better ; but they are not our ways. We are less law-abiding as a nation than New Zealand, and more rampantly independent as individuals. An American community would soon kick holes all through the Acts of Parliament of the other country. We shall have to solve our social problems in our own way, and perhaps after longer and severer experiences than those of the colony. ' An ideal laboratory ' is what a canny Scotch Labour leader called New Zealand. Such it is, indeed ; and we must consider her legislation as laboratory experiments for ourselves." I have to add only two statements. One is that during my visit I was met by unfailing courtesy on the part of all persons from which I sought information ; especially by Sir Joseph Ward, to whom I am indebted for most of the local statistical information used in this paper. When speaking on the same subject, Dr. Victor S. Clark said, " New Zealand is a country that one delights to visit and he regrets to leave it. Nature has endowed it with an excellent climate, abundant resources, and beautiful scenery. The people are of selected stock and of our nearest kin. Nowhere will a stranger meet with sincerer courtesy or more cordial hospitality. One feels like making a general acknowledgment to the whole colony for kindnesses received, when he leaves its shores." The other statement will be this : I set out with my paper to show—and I think that I have shown—that if the natural resources of New Zealand are an unmeasurable quantity, if the yeoman character of the people touches the highest mark, and if the communal government of the country falls

short only of the miraculous, the climatic conditions of the country
generally are most favourable to field industries, that they very
largely contribute to individual and public prosperity ; and that,
therefore, in these respects New Zealand is favoured above all the
other islands and the mainland of Australasia.

ETHNOLOGICAL NOTES ON THE ABORIGINAL TRIBES OF WESTERN AUSTRALIA.[*]

By R. H. MATHEWS, L.S.,

Associe. etranger Soc. d'Anthrop. de Paris.

SYNOPSIS.—Prefatory; Origin of Australian Aborigines; Rock Pictures; Organisation; Initiation Ceremonies; Extraction of Teeth; Superstitions, etc.; Description of Plates; Language; Vocabularies.

During several years past I have been endeavouring to obtain reliable details of the rock-pictures and some other customs of the aboriginals of Western Australia. My mode of procedure has been to write to the owners and managers of stations in different parts of that State, to members of the Police Force, and also to others who might be recommended by any of these. Many of the persons who were thus communicated with made no response, but an individual observer here and there took an interest in my work, and did his best to help me.

I supplied to my correspondents categorical lists of the particulars required, and when I received a reply showing that the writer was a capable man, I again wrote to him for further details, or respecting new matters suggested by his letter. From the reliable character of my correspondents, and my own general knowledge of the subject under discussion, I feel sure that the information supplied in this article can be relied upon.

ORIGIN OF THE AUSTRALIAN ABORIGINES.

The probable origin of the Australian aborigines, and the development of some of their customs, are dealt with in my article[†] on "Les Indigènes d'Australie," contributed to the twelfth session of the International Congress of Prehistoric Anthropology and Archæology, held at Paris in 1900, and therefore it has not been thought necessary to say anything on that subject in the present paper.

ROCK PICTURES,

The rock-pictures of Western Australia, like those of New South Wales, must be divided under two heads—Carvings and Paintings. In the former the drawings are cut into the surface of the rock

---

[*] Read before the Royal Geographical Society of Australasia, Queensland.

[†] Congrès Internat. d'Anthrop. et d'Archéol. préhist., Compte Rendus 12me Session, pp. 488-495. Also see my article in L'Anthropologie, vol. xiii., pp. 233-240.

either in outline or in low relief, whilst in the latter the pictures are painted in pipe-clay, red-ochre, or charcoal on the walls or roofs of caves or sheltered places, protected from the weather by overhanging ledges of rock.

Rock Carvings.—The mode of executing these carvings is as follows:—The outline of some object, say a kangaroo, was first sketched or designed on a smooth or even-faced rock, selected on account of its suitability for the purpose. Then the operator got a piece of hard stone, broken or chipped to a point or edge, with which he chopped and battered at the surface of his design until all the space inside the outline had been beaten away to a fairly uniform depth, say from a sixteenth of an inch to a quarter of an inch. The new surface exposed in this way forms a striking contrast to the surrounding weathered exterior of the rock. This fresh surface retains a distinctive colour for a long period, and shows the figures very clearly, giving them, at a distance, the appearance of standing out in relief.

The hammering and beating process is generally continued all over the surface of the design, but in some instances a band or groove is first formed along the outline of the figure, by chopping and hammering the rock surface in the way above described. The artist could then either batter away the internal surface, or leave the drawing in outline only.

It will be observed that the above method of indenting the design upon the rock differs somewhat from that employed in New South Wales, which I have described elsewhere.* In the counties of Cumberland, Hunter, and other places on the coast of New South Wales, where rock-carvings abound, the rocks consist of Hawkesbury sandstone, in which lines and grooves could be cut with comparative ease. In many parts of Western Australia, however, on the Upper Murchison, Gascoyne, Ashburton, Fortescue, Yule, and other rivers, for example, the rocks are mostly granite and basalt, to make marks on which would be very difficult. Repeated blows, as above described, would be the only way to execute the work with such rude tools as those used by the aboriginal artists.

About two miles south-westerly from Mount Stewart Station, on the Ashburton River, there are some hills, abounding in denuded masses of granite projecting many feet above the ground. Under overhanging ledges of these rocks, and in disintegrated hollows in their sides, the natives have apparently taken shelter from the sun and rain. On the walls of the rock-shelters, as well as on neighbouring rocks exposed to the weather, there are figures of men, iguanas, and other animals, all executed by beating away the surface

---

* "The Aboriginal Rock Pictures of Australia."   Proc. Roy. Geo. Soc. Australasia, Queensland. Vol. x., pp. 54-56.

of the rock within their outline. There is no proportion between the relative sizes of the objects depicted; for example, there are drawings of men from one foot six inches to three feet, while iguanas on the same rock are as large as the men. Pictured rocks of this kind are usually near rock-holes, or other places containing water, which form convenient camping localities for the natives. Similar drawings to those described, incised in the rocks in the same manner, are found in several places throughout the Ashburton district.

On Hillside Station, between the Shaw and De Grey rivers, are some large granite rocks, close to the homestead, on which are drawn several pictures by cutting or beating away the surface of the rock. One of these represents a man about seven feet high.

Rock carvings are very numerous on the Yule and Shaw rivers, and, as one of my informants puts it, "they are in a variety of vulgar attitudes." They are incised on basaltic and granitic rocks by battering constantly within the margin of the object outlined until a slight depression is worn in the rock. Such drawings retain their fresh appearance for a very long time.

Similar carvings to the foregoing are reported by my correspondents as existing on Fortescue, Lyndon, Gascoyne, and Murchison rivers.

By far the most interesting and numerous display of aboriginal rock carvings in Western Australia, are found on Depuch Island, situated opposite Balla Balla, a small town formed, during recent years, on the mainland. The island is about four miles distant from the shore, and about six miles from Balla Balla township. The shores of the mainland in that locality consist of low banks of mud and sand, studded with mangroves. At low water spring-tides these sandbanks are sufficiently dry in some places, to admit of the natives walking out to the island, which is called, in their language, Wommalunna.

The island is a little over three miles long, and upwards of two miles wide. The highest part is at the western end, where it attains an elevation of between 500 and 600 feet. On the eastern end of Wommalunna is a fresh water spring, or natural tank, close to which are the native drawings described in this article. In rainy weather, water also collects in hollows in the rocks at different places. The natives used to cross over to the island, and remain there as long as the water lasted.

The island is one huge mass of igneous rocks, standing on end in thin layers, piled so loosely, block upon block, that in climbing over them, one expects the touch of his feet to start some monolith thundering down into an adjacent gully. Even the hardy spinnifex cannot grow excepting in the gullies, where a few stunted white gum-trees and scrubs are also to be found. This scanty vegetation, however, sustains numbers of rock wallabies.

It will give the reader some idea of the great number of these rock pictures if I quote Mr. H. A. Hall's answer to my request to try and count them : " It would take hours to discover and count approximately all the drawings in the one gully I examined, still I think it is safe to say there are about a hundred. But there are many gullies on the island, and I am led to believe there are drawings more or less, in most of them. In fact, a week or ten days could easily be spent in making up records of the aboriginal work." Mr. Wm. Byron, in one of his letters says, " After some difficulty I am able to send you about forty copies of the rock carvings on Depuch Island, of which there are hundreds."

In May and June, 1840, Captain Wickham, in the surveying ship *Beagle*, was in the vicinity of Depuch Island, the position of which he gives as Lat. 20° 38′ S., and Long. 117° 44′ E. Both he and Captain Stokes subsequently described the aboriginal drawings discovered there.* Captain Wickham speaks of " the vast number of specimens of art," and Captain Stokes says, " the number of specimens is immense," showing that both these officers were impressed with the great profusion of the drawings. Captain Stokes adds : " There is not in them to be observed the slightest trace of indecency." He either did not see the pictures found by my correspondents, or he mistook them for saurians—a mistake which anyone unacquainted with aboriginal drawings would be likely to make, especially in regard to some of them, where the penis is so much elongated as to resemble a tail ; and in others where the length of the body is out of proportion to the rest of the figure. In fig. 6, however, of his plate of drawings, Captain Stokes shows a man with the genital appendage.

All the native pictures on Depuch Island (Wommalunna), are executed in the manner described in earlier pages of this article—that is, they are incised on the rock by repeated blows with a sharp instrument.

Rock Paintings.—The rock paintings of Western Australia are produced mainly by drawing the required object on the smooth surface of the rock in the required colour. In some cases the objects are shown in outline only ; in other instances the space within the outline is painted with a wash of the same tint ; whilst not infrequently this space is shaded by lines or dots drawn either all in the same colour, or in two or more different tints. The drawings which appear in red are no doubt done with red oxide of iron, found as a clay, and known as red ochre. The white colour would be either pipeclay or fine ashes from the camp fire ; whilst the black drawings are done with charcoal or soot.

---

* Capt. Wickham, "Notes on Depuch Island," Journ. Roy. Geog. Soc. (London, 1842), vol. xii., pp. 78-83.

Captain Stokes, "Discoveries in Australia" (London, 1846), vol. ii., pp. 168-172.

Native paintings consist largely of representations of the human hand. In some instances the extended hand was placed firmly on the surface of a rock sheltered from the weather, and the required colour blown or squirted over it out of the mouth. In other cases the palm of the hand of the artist was either rubbed over with a liquid, or was dipped into it, and while wet was closely pressed against a smooth surface on the cave wall. Upon removing the hand, the coloured impression of it was left clearly defined on the rock. Occasionally the surface of the rock was coloured previous to making the paintings upon it, for the purpose of greater artistic effect.

On the Ord River, Hall's Creek, Margaret River, and Sturt Creek, Mr. J. Wilson informs me there are numerous paintings on the rocks, representing kangaroos, snakes, iguanas, human feet, etc. Mr. J. C. Rose states that paintings of human figures, crocodiles, reptiles, and other animals, as well as native weapons, are common on the Fitzroy, Fraser, and Lenard rivers. I learn also from Mr. E. Smith, Mr. J. Hancock, and others, that aboriginal paintings on the rocks are plentiful on the Upper Murchison, Ashburton, Fortescue, and other rivers, being usually found near water. They consist of men, hands, weapons, snakes, and other devices.

The most famous of Western Australia's paintings, and at the same time amongst those possessing the greatest interest, are those discovered by Capt. Grey, afterwards Sir George Grey, on the Glenelg River, in March, 1838, which were described and illustrated in a work written by him in 1841.* Nothing definite was again heard of similar paintings in that district till 1891, when Mr. Joseph Bradshaw drew attention to the subject in a paper read before the Geographical Society in Melbourne.†

But the matter was not lost sight of by the Government of Western Australia, and when, in 1901, an expedition was sent out, under the command of Mr. F. S. Brockman, to explore the northwest district of Kimberly, the party was supplied with photographic appliances to secure copies of any cave paintings met with in any part of the journey. At different places photographs were taken, showing some very important aboriginal drawings found on the walls of rocks protected from the weather by overhanging masses of sandstone. The photographs thus obtained have recently been published by the Government of Western Australia‡ in official form.

* Two Expeds. N.-W. and W. Australia (London, 1841), vol. i., pp. 201-218, with six plates.

† Proc. Roy. Geog. Soc. Aust., Victoria Bch., vol. ix., p. 100, with one Plate. See also Journ, Anthrop Inst., London, vol. xxiii., Plates 5 and 6.

‡ Report on Exploration of North-west Kimberley (Perth, 1902), pp. 4, 6, 7, 12, 18. Plates 4, 5, 6, 10, 12, 13, 15-20, 23-26.

Several of the paintings discovered by Mr. F. S. Brockman and his party are similar in character to those reported by Capt. Grey, and in order to give this matter further publicity, I have thought it desirable to copy one of the recent photographs into this article, because the Journal of this Society will go into many channels which will not be reached by the report of Mr. Brockman's discoveries.

The figure I have chosen for reproduction is numbered Plate 17 in Mr. Brockman's report. This painting is one of several discovered in caves on Bachsten Creek, a tributary of the Calder River, which empties into Collier Bay. This figure is all painted in red colour, with the exception of the eye-balls and the pendant-like object on the chest, which are in black, the whole of the rock-surface having been previously coloured white. The outlines of the face were measured, and found to be eighteen inches long and twelve inches broad. The entire painting is about five feet high.

The face is bounded by a double line, which extends downwards to form the shoulders, and is continued across the breast. The countenance consists of very large eyes and nose, but no mouth, unless the lower portion of the nose be intended for that feature. Around the sides and top of the head is a sort of halo, with lines radiating through it from the head outwards. Just beyond the halo is a broad band with a number of spots at tolerably regular intervals along the middle of it; and the ends of this band, which appear to be tasselled, almost touch the shoulders. There are two short arms, with bands around them, and five fingers on each hand. In the centre of the chest is a black object, the vertical dimension of which is about double the horizontal. The entire painting terminates at about the waist or abdomen, and there is nothing by which the sex can be determined. The vertical lines drawn on the body from the thorax downwards are not in my opinion intended to represent clothing, but are only for ornamentation. Towards the right of the picture are some rude outlines, one of which resembles a human foot with four toes, painted in red colour.

Somewhat similar paintings were found by Mr. Brockman's party in different places in the Kimberly district, but space precludes more than this brief mention of them. Plate 16 of Mr. Brockman's report represents a number of hands stencilled on a cave wall, similar to those reported by me to the Anthropological Society at Paris in 1898.*

---

* "Gravures et Peintures sur Rochers par les Aborigènes d'Australie," Bull. Soc. d'Anthrop. de Paris, t. ix, 4me Serie, pp. 425-432.

ORGANISATION.

Western Australia is the largest of all the Australian States, and its native inhabitants have several systems of social organisation, which I will briefly refer to, for the purpose of giving their geographic distribution.

The most primitive of these organisations is the *Túar* system which exists among the tribes on the west coast about Dongarra northerly to Onslow. In this system, the elders of the tribe allot the progeny of certain women to be the wives of certain men, but the relationship existing between the parties to the marriage must not be nearer than that of second cousins. As the *Túar* is the same in principle as the *Nanarri* system of New South Wales, described by me in a previous paper in 1900,* it will not be necessary to go into details here.

Proceeding southerly from Dongarra to Perth and Albany, and thence to Eucla, extending inland to Norseman and Lake Barlee, we find the people of each tribe divided into two intermarrying phratries, called Wurtungmat and Munnitchmat, with rules of marriage and descent in accordance with the following table:—

TABLE 1.

Phratry.	Father.	Mother.	Offspring.
A	Munnitchmat	Wurtungmat	Munnitchmat
B	Wùrtungmat	Munnitchmat	Wurtungmat

Mr. Thos. Muir, J.P., of Deeside Station, Western Australia, supplied this information in response to a letter which I wrote him. On my writing again, requesting him to further check the descent of the offspring, his reply was " this table is exactly right."

The families composing the two primary divisions mentioned bear the *totem* names of different animals, plants, or inanimate objects. Among the totems of the Munnitchmat phratry may be mentioned the following:—White cockatoo, kangaroo, fire, common black and white magpie, dog, pelican, carpet-snake, kangaroo-rat, blow-fly, porcupine, parakeet, and pigeon.

The undermentioned totemic names may be enumerated as embracing some of the people of the Wurtungmat phratry:—Crow, bandicoot, emu, mopoke, ringtail opossum, chuick (bird), black duck, black cockatoo, iguana, spear, lizard, turkey, and wallaby.

My enquiries respecting the line of descent of the totems has not yet been satisfactory, but I am following up the investigation.

Another form of organisation consists in the bi-section of each phratry, thus making four intermarrying divisions, called Bulcharri, Kurrimurra, Burronga, and Banaka, or dialectical variations of these

---

* Journ. Roy. Soc. N.S. Wales, xxxiv, pp. 263-264.

names. This system is in operation over more than half the geographic area of Western Australia, together with a wide zone through the centre of South Australia, reaching as far as the Georgina River, on the frontier of Queensland.

In all the northern part of Western Australia, situated north-easterly of a line drawn approximately from Collier Bay to Lake Macdonald, and continuing eastward into the Northern Territory, each phratry is subdivided into four sections, thus making eight divisions of the community. The names of these divisions are given in Table 16, *infra*.

In order to explain this subject, it will be necessary to introduce tables to exhibit the intermarriage of the different divisions, and the sections to which the resulting offspring belong.

On the Murchison, Greenough, Sanford, Roderick, Wooramel, Gascoyne, and Lyons rivers, the several native tribes are divided as in the following table:—

TABLE 2.

Phratry.	Father.	Mother.	Offspring.
A	Bûldyerri Kaimarra	Burung Bugarlu	Bugarlu Burung
B	Burung Bugarlu	Bûldyerri Kaimarra	Kaimarra Bûldyerri

These sectional names, with some modifications, are found among the natives at Weld Spring, Bonython Creek, Lake Throssall, Elder Creek, Glen Cumming, and extend eastward into South Australia, where a similar organisation exists among the Andikariña and Arrinda tribes.

The tribes on the Ashburton, Fortescue, Oakover, and Throssell rivers have similar section names, with the exception that Banaka takes the place of Bugarlu, as under:—

TABLE 3.

Phratry.	Father.	Mother.	Offspring.
A	Bulcharri Kurrimurri	Burronga Banaka	Banaka Burronga
B	Burronga Banâka	Bulcharri Kurrimurri	Kurrimurri Bulcharri

These sections reach easterly into the Northern Territory of South Australia.

In the Roeburne district, and on the Yule, Maitland, Shaw, and De Grey rivers, the natives have practically the same four names for the divisions, but the sections constituting the phratries are different, as shown in the following table:—

TABLE 4.

Phratry	Father	Mother	Offspring
A	Paldyarri Burungo	Kaiamara Banaka	Banaka Kaiamara
B	Kaiamara Banaka	Paldyarri Burungo	Burungo Paldyarri

On the Lower Fitzroy and Lennard rivers, Jurgurra Creek, and thence along the coast to Broome and Condon, are a number of tribes possessing the following four section names, which differ but slightly from those in the other tables:—

TABLE 5.

Phratry	Father	Mother	Offspring
A	Parradyerri Parungo	Kaiamba Panaka	Panaka Kaiamba
B	Kaiamba Panaka	Parradyerri Parungo	Parungo Parradyerri

It will be observed in Tables 4 and 5, that Paldyarri and Burungo constitute Phratry A, whereas in Tables 2 and 3, that phratry consists of Buldyerri and Kaimara. This matter will be again referred to farther on.

Among a number of tribes occupying the country drained by the Ord, Denham, Fitzroy, and Margaret rivers, and on Sturt Creek, the people are classified into eight sections, which intermarry in conformity with fixed laws. A name is given to each of the sections, by means of which the members of the different divisions are readily distinguished; and identification is further facilitated by a masculine and feminine form of each of these eight names. Table 16.

The division into eight sections is also in operation over the greater portion of the Northern Territory, and extends into the north-west corner of Queensland.[1] From information supplied by Mr. J. Cahill, manager of Wave Hill Station, on Victoria River, I reported the names of the eight sections obtaining on that river and its affluents with the laws of intermarriage and descent.[2]

Mr. W. Holze, of Daly Waters, in 1900 gave me full details of the intermarriages of the eight sections of the Chingalee tribe, and likewise of the tribe at Elsey Creek. I contributed the former to the Anthropological Society at Washington,[3] and the latter I reported to

[1] See my paper on "Native Tribes of Queensland," American Anthropologist, vol. i. New Series, pp. 595-597.

[2] "Divisions of Tribes in the Northern Territory," Journ. Roy. Soc. N.S. Wales. xxxiii., p. 112. Queensland Geog. Journal, xvi., p. 72.

[3] American Anthropologist, ii., N.S., pp. 494-497.

the Royal Society of New South Wales the same year.[1] I also communicated the divisions of the Elsey Creek tribe to the Society of Anthropology at Paris.[2]

Mr. Holze sent me a comprehensive vocabulary of the Chingalee language, and also a valuable table of totems, showing their inter-marriage and descent, both of which I contributed to the Royal Geographical Society at Brisbane in 1901.[3] I am likewise indebted to Mr. Holze for much reliable and important information respecting native customs in the Northern Territory.

The eight sections of the M'Arthur and Calvert rivers tribes were collected for me by Mr. M. Costello, and communicated to the American Philosophical Society at Philadelphia in 1899.[4]

The Inchalachee and Warkya (or Waggaia) tribes have eight divisions, which were tabulated under my direction by Mr. A. H. Glissan, Rockland Station, and reported by me in 1899.[5]

In the foregoing brief review of the social organisation of the native tribes of Western Australia, it has been shown that in some districts the primitive system of the Túar is employed to regulate intermarriages. In other localities the community consists of two phratries, as A and B, without any further subdivision. (Table 1). Over the greater part of Western Australia there is a partition of each phratry into two sections, making four divisions of the tribe. (Tables 2, 3, 4, 5). Among the inhabitants of other districts there are four subdivisions of each phratry, giving a total of eight sections. (Table 16).

These different types of organisation have originated so far back in the past that the present natives cannot give any account of their *raison d'être*, and therefore I shall venture to state a theory by means of which the origin of the different systems could be accounted for. My object in adopting this course is to invite discussion on this highly important subject among ethnologists in various parts of the world reached by the Journal of this Society.

---

4 " Marriage and Descent among the Australian Aborigines." Journ. Roy. Soc. N.S. Wales, xxxiv., pp. 130-131.

5 " Organisation Sociale des Tribus Aborigènes," de l'Australia, Bulletins Soc. d'Anthrop. de Paris, t. ii., serie 5, pp. 415-419.

6 " Ethnological Notes on the Aboriginal Tribes of the Northern Territory," Queensland Geogrraphical Journal, xvi., pp. 85-89.

7 " Divisions of North Australian Tribes," Proc. Amer. Philos. Soc., xxxviii., p. 77.

8 Journ. Roy. Soc. N.S. Wales, xxxiii., p. 111. See also my article on " Les Indigènes d'Australie," Congrès Internat. d'Anthrop, et d'Archéol. prébist., Compte Rendu, 12me Sess., p. 492.

Following a line of reasoning I have before adopted,[1] in dealing with Australian organisations, we will assume that in the remote past there were two tribes called Bulcharri and Banaka, who, either by conquest or as a matter of public policy, amalgamated, and that the Bulcharri men married the Banaka women, and *vice versa*. This would give us the organisation shown in the following table, the offspring taking the mother's name:—

TABLE 6.

Phratry.	Father.	Mother.	Offspring.
A	Bulcharri	Banaka	Banaka
B	Banaka	Bulcharri	Bulcharri

Let us also say that Kaimarra and Burungo united in the same manner, and intermarried one with another, as follows:—

TABLE 7.

Phratry.	Father.	Mother.	Offspring.
A	Kaimarra	Burungo	Burungo
B	Burungo	Kaimarra	Kaimarra

It will be observed that the organisation in each of the Tables 6 and 7 is precisely the same in principle as that existing at the present day among the Parnkalla[2] tribe, the Yowerawarraka tribe[3] the Barkunjee tribe[4], and several others. Likewise, the children belonged to the same phratry as their mothers, as in the tribes quoted.

We will now assume that the confederacy represented in Table 6 conquered that in Table 7, or that these two peoples considered it politic to amalgamate for purposes of mutual advantage. Such an alliance could have been accomplished by the interchange of sisters between the members of the opposite confederacies in this way:— Bulcharri could have taken the sister of Burungo, and have given his own sister in exchange; Kaiamarra and Banaka could have exchanged sisters in a similar way; but there was no alteration made in the names of a man's offspring in any instance. The united confederacy would then be illustrated by Table 3, *ante*, which represents the organisation as we find it to-day among the tribes on the Ashburton and other rivers.

On the Murchison River and elsewhere, the section name Bugarlu, as stated in an earlier page, takes the place of Banaka,

1 " The Origin, etc., of the Australian Aborigines," Proc. Amer. Philos. Soc., Philadelphia, vol. xxxix., pp. 556-578, with map of Australia.   Also see my paper in "L'Anthropologie" (Paris, 1902), vol. xiii., pp. 233-240.

2 Proc. Amer. Philos. Soc., Philadelphia, vol. xxxix., p. 82.

3 *Op. cit.*, p. 83.

4 Journ. Roy. Soc. N.S. Wales, vol. xxxii., p. 242.

which could be explained by supposing a tribe named Bugarlu, instead of Banaka, to have amalgamated with Bulcharri in past times.

Further, if we take the four names in Tables 4 and 5, we discover that the phratries comprise different sections to those shown in Tables 2 and 3, as already mentioned in an earlier page. It may be postulated that the people in Table 4, for example, consisted in ancient times of the confederacies illustrated in Tables 6 and 7, and that at a later period they became amalgamated. The consolidation of the four sections, however, was effected by the coalition of different pairs of sections. Bulcharri married the sister of Kaiamarra, and Kaiamarra took the sister of Bulcharri as his spouse; Burungo and Banaka exchanged sisters with each other in the same manner, thus constituting the organisation existing at present on the De Grey River and elsewhere. (Tables 4 and 5).

Instead of exchanging sisters, as above suggested, the coalescence of tribes could be accomplished by the exchange of wives. This arrangement would be only temporary, or it might endure for that generation. But in the rising generation, the men of Phratry A would obtain their wives from among the sisters of the men of Phratry B, and conversely, precisely the same as we find marriages arranged at the present day.

We also discover, in examining Tables 3 and 4, that although the phratries in each table are not composed of the same sections, yet the offspring have the same fathers in both tables. For example, in Table 3, Bulcharrie marries Burronga, and his children are Banaka; but if we take Table 4, it is seen that Bulcharri marries Kaiamurra, and his children still retain the name of Banaka. This is, of course, likewise true of the other three sections.

This may, perhaps, bear the construction that at the time of the amalgamation of these four sections, it was considered best to bestow on a man's offspring the same section name which they bore before the consolidation, or, in other words, not to let the mother influence the line of descent, as had been the custom under the ancient organisation represented in Tables 6 and 7.

Referring back to Phratry A of Table 3, it will be observed that Burronga is the regularly appointed wife of Bulcharri, and his children are Banaka. In certain cases, however, where there is no blood relationship, it is sometimes permissible for Bulcharri to marry a Banaka woman belonging to a distant tribe, but in such case the children are called Burronga. This alternative privilege may be a survival of the archaic law, when Bulcharri married Banaka, as in Table 6, and the descent of the progeny was regulated by the mother. Kaiamarra can, under like circumstances, take a Burronga woman as his alternative wife, and his children are Banaka. The same rule applies to the men in both sections of Phratry B.

The fact of different pairs of sections being employed to constitute the phratries exhibited in Tables 3 and 4, and the consequent variation in the intermarriage of the four sections, together with the persistency of the names of a man's children in both tables, may help to strengthen the hypothesis of the consolidation of a number of small clans into pairs, as in Tables 6 and 7, or into quartettes, as in Tables 2, 3, 4, and 5.

If we travel easterly from the tribes we have been describing, and proceed into the Northern Territory, we find not only the same organisation, but section names are met with, some of which are almost identical with those in Tables 3 and 4. For example, at Charlotte Waters and Alice Springs, in the Northern Territory, the people are segregated into four sections, which intermarry as in the following synopsis :—

TABLE 8.

Phratry.	Father.	Mother.	Offspring.
A	Bultara	Koomara	Panungka
	Parulla	Panungka	Kumara
B	Kumara	Bultara	Parulla
	Panungka	Parulla	Bultara

The sections Bultara, Kumara, and Panunga very closely resemble the corresponding names in Table 4, but Parulla appears in lieu of Burungo. This intrusive name, if it be not a dialectic variation of Burungo, may be accounted for in the same way as Bugarlu, referred to in an earlier page.

Continuing still farther to the eastward till we reach the boundary between the Northern Territory and Queensland, we encounter tribes having four sections, as under :—

TABLE 9.

Phratry.	Father.	Mother.	Offspring.
A	Belthara	Gubilla	Deringara
	Kumara	Deringara	Gubilla
B	Gubilla	Belthara	Kumara
	Deringara	Kumara	Belthara

The two names in Phratry A of this table are substantially the same as Bulcharri and Kaiamurra in that phratry of Table 3, but the two remaining names, Gubilla and Deringara, take the place of Burronga and Banaka.

It now remains to apply our theory to the explanation of the origin of the present system of dividing a tribe into eight sections, the names of which are given in Table 16, *infra*. In order to simplify the illustrations, the masculine form only of each section name will be used.

Let us assume that in times of yore the Changura and Chabalyi clans became consolidated, by conquest or otherwise. A Changura man espoused a Chabalyi woman, and *vice versa*, the offspring taking the name of the mother in both cases, as under:—

TABLE 10.

Phratry.	Father.	Mother.	Offspring.
A	Changura	Chabalyi	Chabalyi
B	Chabalyi	Changura	Changura

A similar incorporation took place between the Chauan and Chauarding tribes:—

TABLE 11.

Phratry.	Father.	Mother.	Offspring.
A	Chauan	Chauarding	Chauarding
B	Chauarding	Chauan	Chauan

Afterwards these two confederacies amalgamated by an interchange of sisters, as exemplified in the attached table, but leaving the section name of the offspring the same as before:—

TABLE 12.

Phratry.	Father.	Mother.	Offspring.
A	Changura / Chauarding	Chauan / Chabalyi	Chabalyi / Chauan
B	Chauan / Chabalyi	Changura / Chauarding	Chauarding / Changura

In those days, Changura had, perhaps, the privilege of taking Chabalyi as an alternative wife, being similar to the law now existing among the tribes on the Ashburton River and other parts of Western Australia, possessing a quadruple organisation, already referred to. Chabalyi was Changura's former wife in Table 10.

In illustrating the remaining four sections, we will postulate that in former days the Chungala and Chambin tribes sought incorporation, and intermarried one with the other, as follows:—

TABLE 13.

Phratry.	Father.	Mother.	Offspring.
B	Chungala	Chambin	Chambin
A	Chambin	Chungala	Chungala

We will also suppose that Chuaru and Chagara were similarly coalesced:—

TABLE 14.

Phratry.	Father.	Mother.	Offspring.
B	Chuaru	Chagara	Chagara
A	Chagara	Chuaru	Chuaru

Subsequently these two confederacies became amalgamated in the same manner as those represented in Table 12, the section name of each man's children remaining unchanged:—

TABLE 15.

Phratry.	Father.	Mother.	Offspring.
B	Chungala	Chuaru	Chambin
	Chagara	Chambin	Chuaru
A	Chuaru	Chungala	Chagara
	Chambin	Chagara	Chungala

From eight separate clans or tribes we have now illustrated the development of two communities, one represented by Table 12 and the other by Table 15, each of which has four intermarrying divisions in its social organisation. At a later period these two communities became consolidated into their present form, and the hypothetical course followed in arriving at this result will now be investigated:

A man of the Changura section in Table 12 espoused the sister of Chungala in Table 15; Chauan took the sister of Chuaru; Chagara in Table 15 annexed the sister of Chabalyi; and Chambin took the sister of Chauarding. Again, a Chungala man took the sister of Changura; Chauaru espoused the sister of Chauan; Chauarding took the sister of Chambin; and Chabalyi annexed the sister of Chagara. The intermarrying sections of the new organisation, with the names of their sons and daughters, are as under:—

TABLE 16.

Phratry.	Father.	Mother.	Son.	Daughter.
A	Changura	Nungala	Chabalyi	Nauadyerri
	Chauan	Nuaru	Chauarding	Nabungarti
	Chagara	Nauadyerri	Chuaru	Nuaru
	Chambin	Nabungarti	Chungala	Nungala
B	Chungala	Nangili	Chambin	Nambin
	Chuaru	Nauana	Chagara	Nagara
	Chauarding	Nambin	Chauan	Nauana
	Chabalyi	Nagara	Changura	Nangili

The rules of marriage in the above table are those mostly followed; thus, Changura marries Nungala, which I have elsewhere called the "direct" or "tabular" law. Changura can, in certain circumstances, marry Nuaru, which I have denominated the "alternative" law. It may be explained that Nuaru is Changura's father's sister's daughter, but the relationship must be collateral and not of the full blood. Moreover, Changura may occasionally espouse the sister of Chauan, who was the ancient wife of the Changura section (Table 12), which is probably commemorative of the intermarrying code of that period. This may be called the "rare" or "ancient" law. In earlier pages of this article reference has been made to the privilege of marrying the "ancient" wife in the quadruple organisation. Attention is again drawn to the matter, because if it be a survival of the old law, it may add strength to the theory of the consolidation of small tribes into confederacies in the past.

Again, in examining Table 16, it will be seen that Chauan's "tabular" wife is Nuaru, his "alternative" spouse, Nungala, and his "ancient" wife, Nangili. It therefore appears that Changura and Chauan may exercise their choice over the same two sections of women; and they can also make matrimonial exchanges of their sisters with each other. In other words, Changura and Chauan can mutually exchange either their wives or their sisters. These two men were brothers-in-law under the ancient regime (Table 12), and they are indirectly so still. These remarks apply to Chagara and Chambin, and also to the pairs of sections in Phratry B of Table 16.

In Phratry A of Table 16 it is seen that Nungala is the mother of Nauadyerri, Nauadyerri of Nuaru, Nuaru of Nabungarti, and Nabungarti of Nungala, and this series is repeated in the same order for ever. A similar result is obtained by taking successive generations of the women in Phratry B.

Again, taking Phratry A of Table 16, we observe that Changura is the uncle (mother's brother) of Chambin; Chambin is related in the same manner to Chauan; Chauan is the uncle of Chagara; and Chagara is the brother of the mother of Changura—the latter being the name with which we commenced. This succession of the uncles and nephews is repeated in the same order from generation to generation. This applies also to the men of Phratry B.

If we wish to place together all the women in each phratry to show their order of descent, and if we also desire to demonstrate the lineal succession of the uncles and nephews, then Table 16 is a convenient arrangement of the sections. But if our object be to illustrate the descent of the offspring through the men, then the following classification is preferable:—

TABLE 17.

Moiety.	Father.	Mother.	Son.	Daughter.
A	Changura	Nungala	Chabalyi	Nauadyerri
	Chabalyi	Nagara	Changura	Nangili
	Chauan	Nuaru	Chauarding	Napungarti
	Chauarding	Nambin	Chauan	Nauana
B	Chagara	Naudyerri	Chauaru	Nuaru
	Chuaru	Nauana	Chagara	Nagara
	Chambin	Napungarti	Chungala	Nungala
	Chungala	Nangili	Chambin	Nambin

The reader of this table sees that the men of each pair of sections in Moiety A reproduce themselves in alternate generations; that the men in each pair of sections in Moiety B do likewise; and that the children belong to the same moiety as their fathers. Again, the men of Moiety A are the same as those in Table 12, whilst the men of Moiety B coincide with the names in Table 15. It is, moreover, observed that the "direct," the "alternative," and the "rare" wives all belong to the same moiety in each instance.

Full details of the intermarriage and descent of the sections, with particulars of the totems among a number of neighbouring tribes in the Northern Territory, were supplied in an article I contributed to the Geographical Society of Queensland in 1901, to which the reader is referred.

INITIATION CEREMONIES.

In a strip of country commencing at Cape Arid, and thence along the coast to Albany, Fremantle, and Sharks Bay, to Onslow, extending inland all the way for about a hundred miles or more, it is found that the natives neither circumcise nor subincise. But throughout the whole of the remainder of Western Australia both these rites are practised. As I have elsewhere[1] given tolerably full descriptions of the ceremonies connected with the performance of these mutilations, in the adjoining State of South Australia, they will be passed over at present.

EXTRACTION OF TEETH.

Along the West Australian coast from Roebourne or Condon southerly, via Onslow, Carnarvon, Geraldton, and Fremantle, to Albany, and thence easterly to Eucla, on the South Australian boundary, the custom of taking out a front tooth is not practised. From Derby up along the Fitzroy River and its tributaries to Hall's Creek, thence down the Ord River to Wyndham, and thence round along the coast, via Beagle Bay, to Condon, two front teeth are extracted in some tribes, and in others one tooth. In the central districts of Western Australia the extraction of teeth is also in force.

SUPERSTITIONS, ETC.

The natives of Western Australia, like their confreres in other parts of the continent, have many superstitions. They believe in a number of malevolent spirits, who are always prowling about, more especially at night. They are present in deep waterholes, in whirlwinds, in thunder, in certain scrubby and rocky places, in storms, and elsewhere. They are supposed to have the form of men and animals, and possess purely human traits. There is nothing sacred in their character, although they are said to exercise supernatural

[1] "Phallic Rites and Initiation Ceremonies of the South Australian Aborigines," Proc. Amer. Philos. Soc., xxxix., pp. 622-638.

powers. Instead of endeavouring to prop tiate these mysterious creatures, the men treat them as they would any human foe, and try to scare them away by open acts of defiance, or to counteract their wicked designs by magic.

Respecting the origin of these mystic spirits, the natives do not trouble themselves to formulate any definite idea. Some are supposed to have had an existence coëval with that of the blacks themselves, whilst others are feared because they are the shades of departed enemies. There is no conception of a good or friendly spirit any farther than that some of the ancestors of the tribe will try to favour them by driving food-producing animals into their country.

Their ceremonies refer largely to the supply of food. Each wizard or shaman has his own special occult functions. Some profess to have the power of giving success in the chase, others in fishing, others in making rain to supply them with water in the rock-holes, and so on. On such occasions they repair to a secluded rock, called *tarlo*, which is used only at these ceremonies, and the practitioner rubs or beats the rock with a stone held in the hand, muttering incantations the while.

The natives of Sturt Creek and the Fitzroy and Ord rivers believe that a supernatural monster in serpent form made all the rivers, as he travelled inland from the sea, which is his home. In some districts this creature is known as Ranbul, and in others as Wonnaira.

The natives around Weld Spring have a legend that in the desert country beyond the Parker Ranges there are enormous snakes, called Wonnangura, living in the vicinity of rock-holes and other places where there is water. If a blackfellow wishes to go to a rock-hole or spring to get a drink, it is necessary that one or more of his friends should keep watch, or else these venomous monsters would bite him, or perhaps devour him. Whirlwinds are also said to prevail in that country, which would carry a blackfellow off, and deposit him in some rocky mountain or dense scrub far away in an enemy's country. A whirlwind is supposed to be the tail of a maleficent monster in serpent form.

The boundaries of the hunting grounds of the different tribes are defined by patches of scrub, hills, sandy tracts, or any remarkable natural features. If these are trespassed upon by adjoining tribes, the intruders are driven back by armed force.

A man's weapons, utensils and ornaments belong solely to himself, and at his death are buried with him. Each woman also has her own personal property, which is either interred with her or left at her camp. In the Kimberly district the usual mode of burial is to place the body, wrapped in paper-bark, on a platform of sticks in the branches of a tree. Sometimes in rocky country, the body is laid on a shelf of rock, above which there is a projecting ledge.

Among the Lyndon and Minilya river tribes there is a belief that a creature of malignant power, called Yamaji, comes into the camp at night and carries a man away into the mountains, where he changes his language, and brings him back to the camp. Next morning no one can understand the man who has been treated in this way. Sometimes it is a woman who is taken away by Yamaji. Perhaps this superstition has developed to account for a man or woman losing his or her reason after exposure to thirst, sunstroke, or other hardship.

Some of the natives believe they can delay the setting of the sun by lighting a fire on a high rock, or by fastening a burning stick in the fork of a tree. Having done this they travel as fast as they can towards their camp, apparently believing that they will get there before the darkness sets in.

Mr. H. T. Knight, station manager, Lyndon River, writes to me that one day during a thunderstorm he saw a black woman take her little girl and dip her in a pool, for the purpose of inducing the rain to cease, because it was not wanted just then. In an interview with Mr. G. Buchanan, Flora Valley Station, near Hall's Creek, in the Kimberly district, he told me a similar story. A black woman was stopping in the stable, and during a storm she held her child under the drip from the eaves, to stop the rain, in order that she could get away home to her camp.

In my " Ethnological Notes on the Aboriginal Tribes of the Northern Territory,"[1] I have described their customs in hunting, fishing, and other methods of obtaining food; their camps, vessels, and weapons; some of their superstitions, sorcery, barter, modes of burial, wife stealing, etc. All the particulars given in the work referred to are applicable to the aborigines of the Kimberly district of Western Australia. They are in effect the same race as the natives of the part of the Northern Territory with which I dealt in my former treatise, which can therefore be read in connection with the present article.

In conjunction with the present paper, I would also ask the reader to peruse my treatise on " The Origin, Organisation, and Ceremonies of the Australian Aborigines,"[2] which is accompanied by a map of Australia, showing the geographic distribution of the tribes under each type of social organisation, and exhibiting also the boundaries between those tribes who practise circumcision and subincision, and those tribes among whom neither of these genital rites are in force.

---

1 Queensland Geographical Journal, xvi, pp. 76-85.
2 Proc. Amer. Philos. Soc., Phila., U.S.A., xxxix., pp. 556-578.

DESCRIPTION OF PLATES.

PLATE I.—ROCK CARVINGS.

In this plate I have illustrated nine carvings upon rocks on Depuch Island, called by the aborigines Wommalunna, all of which have been drawn to scale by myself.

Figs. 3, 4, 6, 8, and 9 have been drawn from photographs furnished by Mr. W. A. Hall, already referred to in this paper. Figs. 1, 2, and 5 I prepared from careful sketches and measurements taken by Mr. Hall under my direction.

Fig. 7 was copied by myself, as stated in the text, *infra*.

In Figs. 1, 3, 4, 6, 7, 8, and 9, the whole surface within the margin of the object depicted has been chopped or beaten away, this being indicated by solid colour on the plate. Fig. 5 is in outline only, and Fig. 2 partially so.

Fig. 1.—A man three feet seven inches high. It is executed on the perpendicular face of a rock about forty feet up the side of a steep gorge. Mr. W. A. Hall says in his letter to me of September 16th, 1901, " We tried very hard to photograph this figure, but there was too much angle from either side, and only the smallest of ledges in front. The original artist must have suffered some little inconvenience to execute his drawing."

Fig. 2 represents a human foot, with eight toes. It is one foot five inches in length, and seven inches wide. The figure is in outline, with the exception of the toes, where the rock surface has been beaten away.

Fig. 3 shows three birds, cut upon a monolith lying on the side of a hill, and forming an inclination of about forty-five degrees to the horizon. The birds are shown on the plate in their correct relative position to each other, and the line around them represents the margin of the rock on which they are carved. Mr. W. A. Hall says in his letter above mentioned: " The block of stone containing the three birds weighs between two and three hundredweight. I started two of my crew carrying it to the dingey, but the track was so rough, and the tide receding so fast, we had to leave it, but I intend scouring it at some convenient time later on."

Fig. 4 is probably an emu or native companion in the attitude of feeding, and measures two feet three inches from the bill to the tail.

Fig. 5.—This carving is in outline only, the incised lines being about half an inch wide and a quarter of an inch deep in the centre. It is probably an unfinished drawing.

Fig. 6.—This is intended for either a wallaby or kangaroo, and is one foot seven inches in length.

PLATE I.

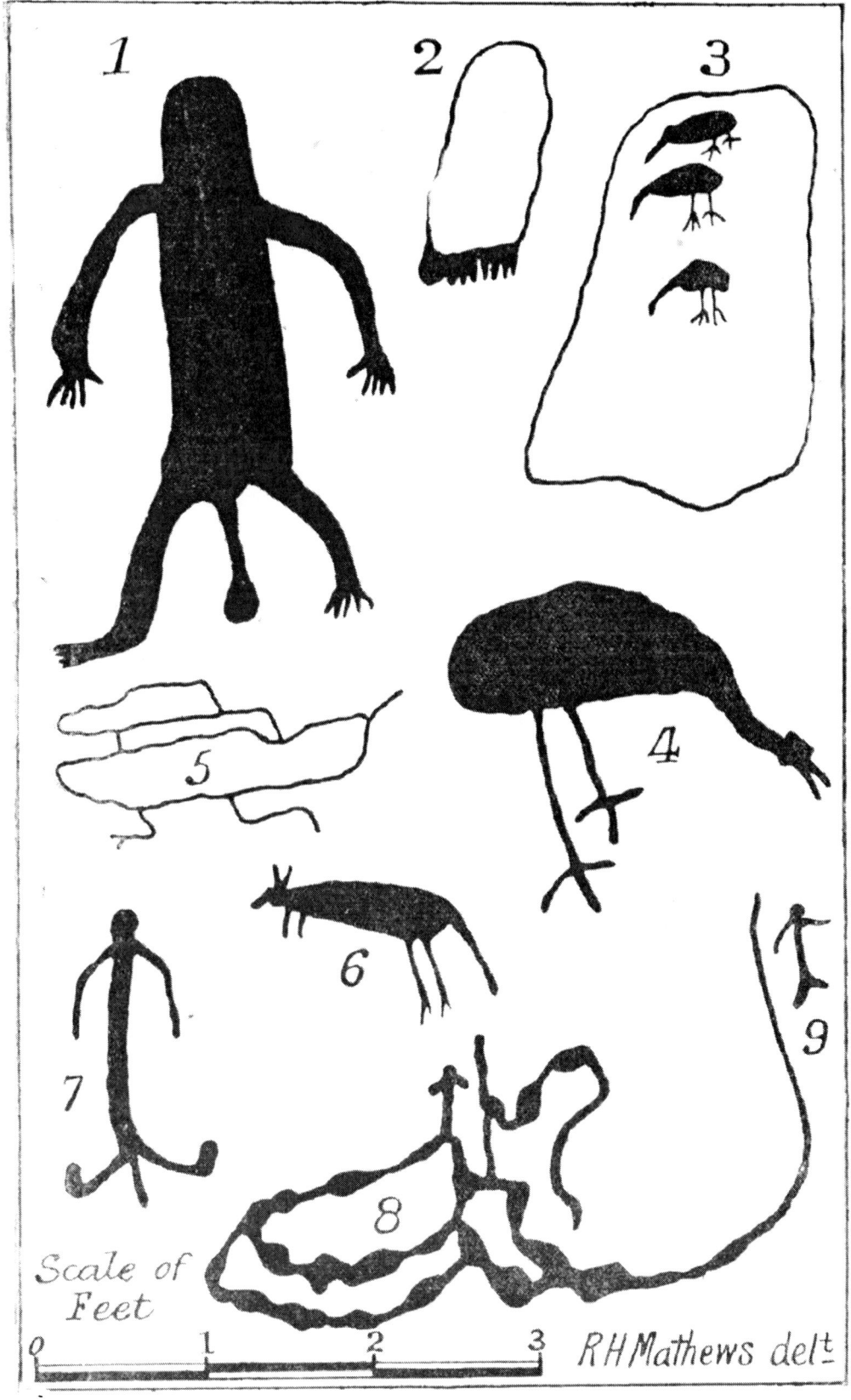

Scale of Feet

0   1   2   3

R H Mathews delt.

Fig. 7 represents a man one foot nine and a-half inches in height, carved on a slab of stone two feet five inches high, by an extreme width of one foot ten inches.

Mr. W. A. Hall brought this rock, which weighs about two hundredweight, with him from Depuch Island to Cossack. On my expressing a wish to see it, he packed it carefully in bags and shipped it to Sydney, whence I had it brought to Parramatta by a drayman. I then copied Fig. 7, which is the only drawing upon this monolith.

Fig. 8.—It is impossible to say what the native artist wished to portray in this drawing, which is on the perpendicular face of a slab of rock.

Fig. 9 is shown in its correct relative position, and represents a man or woman seven and a half inches in length.

It may be stated here that I supplied my correspondents with accurate copies of the carvings published by Capt. Wickham and Capt. Stokes respectively, already referred to, and asked them to endeavour to identify some or all of such drawings. I regret to say that very little success was met with. Fig. 6 of my plate, however, is probably identical with Fig. 11 of Capt. Stokes' plate. or Fig. 67 of Capt. Wickham's plate.

PLATE II.—ROCK PAINTINGS.

The drawings shown on this plate have already been described in the text of this article. from details supplied by Mr. F. S. Brockman, in a personal letter, at my request.

LANGUAGE.

Two short vocabularies are added, for comparison with those compiled by other authors in different parts of Western Australia. The first one contains 155 words noted down by myself from the mouth of a native of the Roebourne district named "Baibung." He belonged to the section Banaka, and totem kangaroo. (See Table 4). The second vocabulary of 125 words is prepared from information supplied to me by Mr. A. E. Clifton, manager of the Yeeda Station, near Derby, and represents the language spoken on the Lower Fitzroy River. In a paper contributed to the Royal Society of New South Wales in 1901, I furnished a vocabulary showing 120 words of the Kishu language. collected under my direction by Mr. W. J. Wilson, police officer at Hall's Creek, in the Kimberly district.[1]

As far as my information at present extends in regard to the languages of Western Australia. I am led to the following conclusions respecting their grammatical structure:—There are the singular, dual, and plural numbers. Nouns and adjectives are declined by postfixes. Pronouns and other parts of speech subject to inflection

---

[1] Journ. Roy. Soc. N.S. Wales, xxxv., pp. 220 222.

have an inclusive and exclusive form of the first person in the dual and plural. The verbs are inflected somewhat similarly to those in the languages of the Darling River tribes in New South Wales.

The study of the aboriginal languages of Western Australia has been very much neglected. The following is a summary of the principal pioneers in this direction :—

In 1842, Mr. Charles Symmons, Protector of the Aborigines, with the assistance of F. F. Armstrong, the Native Interpreter, published

PLATE II.

Rock Paintings.

a short article entitled " Grammatical Introduction to the Study of the Aboriginal Language of Western Australia." It appeared in C. Macfaull's " Western Australian Almanac for 1842, with Appendix," pp. 1-28. This work, which is elementary and incomplete, deals with " the language spoken by the Australian aborigines on the banks of the Swan River, and in the country adjacent."

Mr. Symmons is the only author, so far as I am aware, who has attempted to define the grammatical constitution of the Western Australian tongues. But a few of the vocabularies which have appeared at different times are deserving of mention :—

Captain Grey, afterwards Sir George Grey, prepared a vocabulary of the language spoken " from King George's Sound to more than one hundred miles beyond Perth." The title of this work is " Vocabulary of the Dialects of South-western Australia." (Perth, 1839.)

The Rev. J. Brady printed a " Descriptive Vocabulary of the Native Language of Western Australia." (Rome, 1845.) He explains that " the words contained in this vocabulary are used in the vicinity of Perth and adjacent districts." He also states, " Nothing is said here about the grammar of the language, because it is not sufficiently known."

In 1866, Mr. E. M. Curr published vocabularies of several tribes on the western and southern coasts of Western Australia. " The Australian Race," vol. i, pp. 292-406.

A short vocabulary of native words in use among the Gualluma tribe, located between the Yule and Fortescue rivers, was collected by Mr. E. Clement in 1899, and published in the Journal of the Anthropological Institute (London), vol. ii, N.S., pp. 192-196.

CONCLUSION.

It is hoped that the information supplied in the foregoing pages may be found useful to ethnologists, geographers and linguists in dealing with the customs, boundaries, and classification of Australian tribes.

The attention of the reader is also invited to the following papers contributed by me during past years to other learned societies on the subject of the aborigines of Western Australia.

" Divisions of Some West Australian Tribes," American Anthropologist (Washington, 1900), vol. ii., N.S., pp. 185-187.

" Wombya Organisation of the Australian Aborigines," Ibid., pp. 494-501.

" Some Aboriginal Tribes of Western Australia," Journal Royal Society, New South Wales (Sydney, 1901), vol. xxxv., pp. 217-222.

" Native Tribes of Western Australia," Proc. Amer. Philos. Soc. (Philadelphia, 1900), vol. xxxix., pp. 123-125.

" Western Australian Divisions," Journ. Roy. Soc. N. S. Wales (Sydney, 1898), vol. xxxii., pp. 84-86.

" The Origin, Organisation, and Ceremonies of the Australian Aborigines," Proc. Amer. Philos. Soc. (Philadelphia, 1900), vol. xxxix., pp. 556-578, with map of Australia, on which is shown the distribution of the tribes of Western Australia.

VOCABULARY—ROEBOURNE DISTRICT.

FAMILY TERMS, ETC.

A man, Ngaiada or Mulba.
Husband, Ngurra.
Father, Mamana.
Boy, Kobbodya.
Elder brother, Gurannha.
Woman, Dhurramba.

Old woman, Munga.
Young woman. Kuri.
Wife. Mirrawai.
Sister. Konnarung.
Child, neuter. Munggula.

NATURAL OBJECTS.

Sun, Yunda.
Moon, Willara.
Stars, Binderi.
Pleiades, Kuriguri.
Wind. Thura.
Whirlwind. Wunnangurra.
Thunder, Yindarra.
Lightning. Wulliwuddi.
Clouds. Kandera.
Rain, Yungo.
Water, Baba.
Fire, Kulla.

Camp. Nyirrang.
Bough hut. Maia.
Stone, Munda.
Sand. Yundaga.
Egg. Dyimbu.
Charcoal, Dyinda.
An enemy, Dyuna.
Evil spirit. Warungga.
Any tree. Barku.
Firewood, Thamara.
Flesh, food. Mundu.
Yams. Mudumuri.

PARTS OF THE BODY.

Head. Thuru.
Beard, Nganga.
Hair. Kulkara.
Neck, Ngulye.
Eye, Thula.
Nose. Mula.
Teeth, Era
Tongue, Yaluru.
Ear. Gulga.
Arm. Thilli.
Elbow. Wungulla.
Hand. Murra.
Navel. Nilu.
Stomach. Ngalu.

Ribs, Thambi.
Heart, Kurrunggulla.
Breasts. female. Bebi.
Backbone, Muru.
Thigh or leg. Wulugali.
Foot. Dyinna.
Penis, Wandi.
Scrotum, Karru.
Vulva, Minni.
Bone, Kudyi.
Skin, Kunnu.
Blood, Mudda.
Excrement. Guna.
Urine. Kumbo.

ANIMALS.

Dog, Yugurra.
Wild dog, Wundya.
Kangaroo. Mungurru.
Padamelon, Burtkarri.
White cockatoo. Metameta.

Elack duck, Kundarri.
Corella. Bilyago.
Fish, collectively, ta-wu-ru.
Snakes, collectively, Wallu.
Common lizard, Babangurra.

ANIMALS—*Continued.*

Claw of dog, etc., Birrigal.

Claw of bird, Mungulla.

Common ants, Waruma.

Butterfly, Kunullawulli.

Feathers, Wullaguru.

Shield, Yarra.

Stone knife, Kundi.

Catch, Dagalgo.

Shout, Eramaga.

Smell, Bandilgo.

Bring, Kurrima.

Roast, Thamera.

Walk, Yannambe.

Run, slowly, Winbai.

Run, fast, Murianbai.

Strike, Gurramunbi.

Sit, Bandiamba.

Lie, Ngari.

Cut open, Diagalma.

Go away, Bungarra.

Throw, Ngaialgo.

Flies, Wurri.

Mosquito, Kumiñ.

Louse, Kulo.

Centipede, Minnawanggo.

WEAPONS, ETC.

Hair belt, Barawuru.

VERBS.

Come, Kugai.

Bite, Mindhalgo.

Pierce, Kuddhalgo.

Cry, weep, Nguddyinba.

Sleep, Gununba.

Eat, Ngunnamba.

Drink, Bundyalga.

Jump, Mungangurri.

Arise, Karri.

Fight, Kuiramanba.

Dance, Banigo.

Look, Wialgo.

Kill, Nyiddigalma.

Fly, as a bird, Kungurra.

ADJECTIVES.

Tall, Mandibanga.

Short, Thumbaga.

Black, Waru.

Red, Murrara.

Old, Windo.

Dead, Guru.

Hot, Kumbai.

Cold, Nyugga.

Tired, Kundigo.

Little, Kulugulu.

Large, Kutthaguda.

Quick, Wulli.

Slow, Thuragu.

Strong, Nunggo.

Sick, Wirago.

Wicked, Wulkva

Distant, Kuddvaguda.

Stinking, Buka.

One, Igawuda.

Two, Kudhara.

Several, Murru.

MISCELLANEOUS.

I, nguddha. Mine, nguddhagu. Thou, nyinda. Thine, nyindagu. He, nyia. We two, thou and I, ngalli. Those two, numbalu.

Yes, kugu. No, mita. Here, nunno. There, nyinna. I go, nguddha yannamba. We two go, ugalli yannamballi. We all go, nyealu yannambulu. How far, ngani muna.

Since the occupation of the country by European stock, the following names have been invented:—Cattle, billamanba. Horses, yau-a-da. Sheep, kukundyai.

VOCABULARY—LOWER FITZROY RIVER.

FAMILY TERMS, ETC.

Man, Wamba.

Old man, Wadal.

Father, Ibilla.

Elder brother, Bubbala.

Younger brother, Murridyudda.

Husband, Yargu.

Youth, uncircumcised, Dyuggada.

Youth, circumcised, Balalli.

Man, incised, Wongalong

Woman, Dyandu.

Wife, Wangu.

Mother, Kuya.

Elder sister, Warnu.

Younger sister, Nemmera.

Little girl, Kanyarri.

Maid, Warrindyula.

Child, either sex, bubba.

PARTS OF THE BODY.

Head, Nalma.

Hair, Labindyenna.

Eye, Nemilgera.

Ear, Nillabubba.

Nose, Wanaginna.

Smell, Ibbandyun.

Mouth, Nillira.

Teeth, Cherink.

Chin, Temgu.

Cheek, Maila-maila.

Forehead, Cherribil.

Beard, Ngulgu.

Breasts, female, Numibla.

Finger, Wirril.

NATURAL OBJECTS.

Sun, Walga.

Moon, Kerrading.

Stars, Larn.

Cloud, Warragarra.

Sky, Buddarra.

Rain, Whella.

Rainbow, Miding.

Light, Chanera.

Darkness, Yingadi.

Morning, Neimbi.

Day, Dyumbel.

Night, Baian.

Heat, Barra.

Cold, Amini.

Fire, Dyungu.

Water, Whella.

Milk, Numina.

Evil spirit, Bullingun.

Shadow, Nimmeradya.

Wind, Wongal.

Mist, Dyaboera.

Smoke, Dui.

Thunder, Chidama.

Lightning, Pinmuk.

Country, Burra.

Stone, Woningara.

Canoe, Kulbia.

East, Bauna.

West, Kula.

North, Yo-wan.

South, Yanbun.

Subincision, Worral.

Watercourse, Nimmila

Grass, Worra.

Tree or wood, Barlo.

Bark, Kuding.

Camp, Chalbi.

Hut, Maiarra.

Hole, Dabbu.

Lump, Durrug.

Path, Kurdi.

Footmark, Neinbel.

ANIMALS.

Native-dog. Kurrida.

Kangaroo, Baldyering.

Fish generally, Bi.

Opossum. Langura.

Emu, Yulgi.

Iguana, Banne.

Eaglehawk, Kalbedyug.

Crow, Wungina.

Black duck, Warrabaluin.

Plain-turkey, Mongaiera.

Pelican, Maiada.

Laughing jackass, Dyarradyurra.

Native companion, Kargura.

White cockatoo, Ngulagu.

Black cockatoo, Darreal.

Fly. Dumbara.

Mosquito, Nilagul.

Snake, Churra.

WEAPONS.

Wood spear, Minigwal.

Reed spear, Dyennil.

Shield, Karribina.

Boomerang. Chibba.

Club, Marballing.

ADJECTIVES.

Alive, Marbu.

Dead, Kud.

Large, Wida.

Small, Wuba.

Long, Idan.

Short, Wongoela.

Good, Marbu.

Bad. Melu-marbu.

Hungry, Marrinyang.

Thirsty, Barra.

Red. Bul.

White, Dup.

Black, Rauga.

Full. Mera.

Empty, Marrinyang.

Quick, Bulla-bulla.

Slow. Bunga.

Blind, Mulgun.

Deaf, Bubbadarra.

Strong. Cherril.

Weak, Wogala.

Heavy, Duan.

Light, Ngorla.

Afraid, Waddyi.

Sweet, Yarrawin.

Right, Mummeragun.

Wrong, Chuda.

Straight, Charar

Crooked. Chulga.

CORRECTION.

In Vol. xvi. of this Journal, in my "Ethnological Notes on the Aboriginal Tribes of the Northern Territory," p. 70, fourth line from the bottom, after the word "Nambijana," *add* "or Chapota and Nemira, or Changary and Nhermana." These words were inadvertently omitted.

THE ANTARCTIC:

BEING THE ANNIVERSARY ADDRESS TO THE ROYAL GEOGRAPHICAL SOCIETY OF AUSTRALASIA, QUEENSLAND.*

By the Right Hon Sir HUGH M. NELSON, K.C M.G., D.C.L., F.R.G.S., etc,.
President.

LADIES AND GENTLEMEN,

On the occasion of our last annual meeting, I directed your attention to the exploring expeditions that were then at work in the Antarctic regions, and gave you a short *résumé* of the previous history of Antarctica. One of the most pleasing features connected with this subject in recent times is the combined international action of the various countries that have taken part in the work. This modern exploration may be said to have taken its rise from our Geographical Congress held in London about the year 1894; and three of the most important European nations have co-operated in the search for the secrets of that vast ice-bound region. The Germans and the Swedes each sent out exploring parties supplied with the most approved models of ships specially designed for the purpose; and the British, as I pointed out to you, sent out a most fully equipped expedition under the command of Captain Scott, assisted by a party of scientists, most of whom were lent by the Lords of the Admiralty, who have rendered the Geographical and Royal Societies every assistance in their power. Commander Scott obtained from them almost everything he wanted as regards both officers and men, so that the "Discovery," when locked up in the ice, had on board, out of 38 all told, 30 naval officers and men. And here it is fitting that I should mention the loyal co-operation of the Government of the Argentine Republic, for, when requested by the Geographical Society to establish another magnetic station, the request met with a most cordial assent, and one was immediately equipped on a small island off Staten Island, near Cape Horn; so that simultaneous magnetic observations were able to be taken there, and at Bombay, Mauritius, Christchurch, Melbourne, Falmouth, and Kew, as well as on board all the exploring ships. And I may mention another proof of the cordiality of the Argentine Government and people, for, when it appeared that the Swedish

* Delivered at the Annual General Meeting, September 19, 1904.

expedition was in trouble, on account of the leader, Dr. Nordenskiold, failing to return at the time appointed, they sent out one
of their most capable naval officers for the relief of the expedition,
providing a gunboat for the purpose, and were successful in rescuing
the party and bringing them all safe back with their collections of
fossils, etc., to Buenos Ayres. I also mentioned that an expedition
was equipped and sent from Scotland under the command of Mr.
W. S. Bruce.

Now, I dare say, it would be interesting for you to learn something of the fate of these various expeditions so far as our present
information extends. It will be remembered that the "Scotia"
left the Clyde in the early days of November, 1902. She wintered
in the South Orkneys, and returned at the end of the following
November, leaving a small party to carry on meteorological work,
the vessel returning to Buenos Ayres for coal, etc. In February of
the present year the "Scotia" returned to the South Orkneys, and
continued her explorations in the Weddell Sea. They reached
74 deg. 1 min. S., and 22 deg. N., where they were ice-bound. After
getting free, they coasted 100 miles along what the expedition
believes to be the Antarctic Continent, which would thus lie some
600 miles north of the position in which it has been supposed to be.
It is believed that the collections made will prove of great scientific
importance. The "Scotia" returned via the Cape with a very
successful record for her two seasons' work.

Then, with regard to the Swedish expedition, Dr. Nordenskiold's
experiences were probably of a more sensational character than
those of any of the others. The "Antarctic," in which he sailed
became a total wreck, and the crew under Captain Larsen
experienced great hardships. The doctor was not himself on board
at the time the wreck occurred, as he had established himself at a
station in Admiralty Inlet which he named "Snow Hill," whilst
the ship proceeded exploring southward. On January 10th she
experienced a violent gale from the south, which so compressed the
ice that the ice-blocks were piled higher and higher all around the
long-suffering vessel, and the stern was forced upwards more than
four feet. Then there came a huge block of ice loftier than the
others with a long projecting ice-foot under the surface of the
water. The monster struck the ship from beneath, broke the keel,
tore up the bottom planking, bent the propeller shaft, and so
completely squeezed the after-part of the ship that its timbers gave
way and let in floods of water. By great exertions they managed
to keep her afloat for about a month, until at last all hope was gone,
and after transferring to the ice-floe everything that might come in
useful, the moorings were let go, the Swedish flag was hoisted, and
they all stood silently watching how the gallant ship that had braved

so many hard tussles with hustling ice and boisterous waves in Polar seas, both north and south, slowly and solemnly sank into her watery grave. It was not, however, until November, living mostly upon penguins that they were able to find their way to the station at Snow Hill, and by a fortunate circumstance reached there just as the Argentine relief ship under Lieutenant Irizar arrived. The work of the expedition does them great credit, and the leader has been congratulated on having made an eventful discovery, namely, the finding of land plants on the Antarctic continent, which give a clear intimation that there was once a warm tropical climate in these latitudes; and he has further, probably, established another fact, namely, the connection of the Antarctic lands with South America.

The German expedition leaving Kerguelen Island as I previously mentioned, in the end of January, steered eastward of south until they arrived at shoal water before crossing the Antarctic Circle. Here they discovered land by sledging expeditions about 50 miles south from their winter station, where the ship was beset in the ice. This land consists of a volcanic hill which they named "Gaussberg," and some ice-cliffs, the whole being called "Kaiser Wilhelm Land." Their position was on a comparatively shallow bank; and it is considered that this was a specially favourable position for making biological observations. No land observatory. The meterological series of observations will be valuable, and the magnetic observations taken in co-operation with the other stations have special value. When the ice broke up in the summer, 30th January, Dr. Erick v Drygalski sailed several hundred miles westerly; the "Gauss" returned by way of the Cape.

Let us now devote a little attention to the expedition with which we are more immediately connected, and see how Commander Scott and his party spent their second winter, and how they were able at last to escape from the ice and return to their native land. In conveying to you such information as I have, I think I cannot do better than give you a few extracts from Captain Scott's first report, written on arrival at Auckland Islands. . . . In my last we left the "Discovery" ice-bound near the huge volcanic mountains named by Ross, the Erebus and Terror, having just received from the relief ship "Morning" a supply of coal and provisions

Writing from Auckland Island Commander Scott reports:—

"The winter closed in very rapidly after the departure of the 'Morning' on March 2nd, 1903: temperatures fell and the weather became gloomy, but there was little snow. Some ice broke away, but the open water never came nearer than within four or five miles of the ship. The month of March was occupied principally in laying in a store of seal meat and flesh of skua gulls for winter consumption. Fish traps were also set, but though at first these were very successful they soon ceased to provide any substantial addition to our fare. The articles supplied us by the "Morning" consisted principally of tinned vegetables, soups, sauces, herbs, pickles, and bottled fruits. They were not absolutely essential, but they greatly added to our comfort. Of such necessaries as biscuits, oatmeal, flour, and sugar, we had an ample supply, and from this time we ceased altogether to use tinned meats.

" When April came without change in the ice conditions, we were forced to abandon all hope that the ship would be free. The " Discovery " had been prepared for sea, but she was now again dismantled. The winter awning was spread and snow was placed on the decks. We soon came to understand that our second winter was likely to be far pleasanter than our first. Experience suggested numerous ways in which the material comfort of the living quarters could be improved. The men were in excellent spirits, much exercise was taken, and games of hockey, etc., continued until the light failed. But the greatest advances were made in respect to the food and light. It was only after his departure that I fully appreciated how far our wretched cook had gone in spoiling the food. Under new arrangements the food was always appetizing, and though sealmeat was the principal fare, all hands partook of it and continued to enjoy it thoroughly.

" The light provided throughout the second winter was acetylene gas. A stock of calcium carbide had been obtained for the hut, and this was now brought into use with a single burner in each compartment of the living space. The light was brilliant and had a most happy effect on the comfort of the community. This beautiful illuminant is in every respect excellently adapted for use in a Polar winter. Generally speaking, we had less wind in the early winter of 1903 than in the corresponding season of 1902, but in the latter months of 1903 the wind increased considerably, so that the averages for the two seasons differ but little. The temperatures during the latter season have been far lower. I have already remarked that the ' Discovery ' lay in a most sheltered spot. The difference in temperature between a thermometer in the screen and one placed 1½ mile to the south was rarely less than 10 deg. It was in this outer position, in the month of May, that we read the low temperature of 67.7 deg. From this time the temperature rose until it again fell in the spring. We had no heavy gale or snowfall until the second week in June, when a heavy southerly blizzard again buried the ship in drift.

" Ample employment for the men was found in preparing for the spring sledging. This involved much repairing and renewing and some change in design of the equipment. In drawing out plans for the coming sledging season, I thought it wise to fix its conclusion at a comparatively early date, in order that all hands might be available to assist in releasing the ship should the opportunity occur. The date fixed was December 15, as at this time, in 1902, the open water was within nine or ten miles of the ship. In arranging the extended journey, I was confident that without dogs it would be useless to attempt to penetrate further to the south. My experience of the barrier surface and some arithmetic convinced me that a party of men could not hope to reach beyond the farthest point of the previous year, however amply supported. The actual performance of the southern parties completely justified this view. Our course of the previous year had taken us well clear of the land to the south-west; but there remained many points of interest in connection with the junction between the barrier and the land, and especially in connection with some apparent straits which intersected the coastal mountains, and which we had only viewed at a great distance. In the second place, we did not know what lay to the south-eastward. We imagined the barrier to extend almost indefinitely in that direction, but we had no proof. Finally, I thought it possible, with the help of experience, to penetrate considerably further to the westward over the ice-cap of Victoria Land. Our small complement only admitted of two properly-supported journeys and one unsupported journey. I decided that the supported journeys should be to the south-west and west, the unsupported to the south-east. The latter was entrusted to Lieut. Royds, the south-west journey to Lieut. Barne, and I arranged to lead the western party myself.

"The winter passed away with extraordinary rapidity, and without a single case of sickness. With the spring, the whole ship became very busy with immediate preparations for the sledging.

"Lieut. Barne left the ship on Sept. 12, placed a depôt to the south, and returned on Sept. 20. His party included Lieut. Mulock, Quartly, Smythe, Green, and Joyce. They experienced the lowest temperature for a sledging party on record, the thermometer remaining almost continuously below 60 deg., and registering as low as 68 deg. Under these very severe conditions there was only one very severe frost-bite. This was one of Joyce's feet, which on two occasions had to be nursed back to life for more than an hour.

"The western party of last year spent considerable time in crossing a range of foothills 4,000 feet in height. I thought it possible to avoid this, and started on September 9 to find a new route and establish a depôt. The party included Mr. Skelton, Mr. Dailey, Evans, Lashly, and Handsley. We found an easy road up a glacier, and placed the depôt at a height of 2,000 feet, 60 miles from the ship. Returning from this point in three and a-half days, we regained the ship on September 20. We were to some extent sheltered from the extreme cold encountered by the other parties, but the temperature was frequently below 50 deg., and at lowest 59.5 deg. I have mentioned these temperatures, because I believe they are almost, if not quite, without precedent in Polar travel, and they therefore afford the best possible proof of the excellent state of health of the ship's company.

"The extended south-western journey was started on October 6. One of the most important facts discovered on this journey was the movement of Depôt A. The fact admits of no doubt, as the depôt was established on the line of transit of two well-defined peaks. It was found to have moved a distance of 608 yards across the line. This is the only definite measurement of a barrier movement we have obtained. It may be difficult to understand how vast all these ice-problems are to a sledge party endeavouring to solve them. Once amongst the disturbed ice, it may take days to reach a point but a few miles distant. Meanwhile, the party is repeatedly plunged into hollows, where they can see nothing, and the greatest care has to be exercised to avoid dangerous crevasses.

"The western party left the ship on October 12. The main party consisted of myself, Mr. Skelton, Mr. Feather, Evans, Lashley, and Handsley; the supporting party of Mr. Ferrar, Kennar, Weller, Mr. Dailey, Wilkinson, and Plumley. The ascent, which led over the icy surface of a glacier, was in places extremely rough, and we soon had considerable trouble in keeping the sledges in repair. By October 18 we had arrived at a point about 5,000 feet above sea-level, and 80 miles from the ship; but here, discovering that the runners of three out of four sledges were practically disabled, we had no choice but to return to the ship. With a final march of 31 miles, the ship was reached on the night of October 21. I decided to make a fresh start to the west with the main party only, and arranged for Mr. Ferrar to proceed independently with two men, Kennar and Weller. He elected to accompany my party to the summit, and to make his geological examination when returning, at his leisure. Accordingly, I again left the ship on Oct. 26, with repaired sledges and a party of nine. We had further difficulty with the sledges, and were delayed by thick weather and heavy winds, but on November 4 reached a height of 7,200 feet. Here we were forced to remain in camp for six and a-half days, during the whole of which time the wind blew furiously from the summit; the air was thick with driving snow, and the temperature was continuously low. Two attempts were made to start, but frost-bites came so rapidly that we were quickly driven back to our sleeping-bags. Towards the end the very close confinement began to tell on the party, and I had decided to get away at all hazards, when the wind fortunately lulled. We managed to get away, and over the summit, whilst Mr. Ferrar started to descend. We were now at a height of 8,900 feet, at which altitude we continued as we advanced to the west.

"Dr. Koettlitz spent the greater part of the summer in bacteriological work. Mr. Hodgson took advantage of the fine weather to augment his collections. Mr. Ford remained on board as cook and steward. And Dell, who, on account of a wound in his arm, was prevented from sledging, was employed in training the dog-team. The team, which consisted of six young dogs, born in 1902, soon became highly efficient; at first, in supplying the sawing camp, and later, in communicating with the relief ships, they proved of the greatest use. Before leaving the ship, I had seen a large tent made in preparation for the summer work. I directed that this tent, together with the necessary stores and a boat, should be taken to the northward before December 15, that the tent should be erected in a safe spot to leeward of some islets about nine miles from the ship, and that sawing should be commenced near this camp as soon as the officers and men returned from sledging. I have already mentioned that in December, 1902, the open water was close to the islets. My intention to be back by December 15, 1903, was frustrated, and Lieut. Armitage took charge of the operations, but under considerable difficulties, for the open water was not now within 17 miles of the ship or eight of the camp. Under these circumstances, he decided to start sawing near the camp, thinking that the saw-cuts might remain open, although the floes could not be detached till the outer ice had broken away.

"The sawing was commenced on December 18. But shortly after officers and men were divided into three watches of nine, which, by relieving one another, kept one saw continuously at work. The ice was from 7 feet to 8 feet thick, and the greatest length of cut accomplished in a four hours' watch was 40 feet, where as to clear a channel it is necessary to saw approximately four times its length. It was soon discovered, that the saw-cuts, being filled with slush, were rapidly refreezing. The prospect was not inspiriting, yet the work was cheerfully continued.

"I reached the camp on New Year's Eve, and, seeing the futility of the work, which had now been in full swing for more than ten days, arranged to break up the camp and return to the ship. With the exception of Dr. Koettlitz, Mr. Ford, and my own sledge party, all hands were employed on the saw. The work was hard, and its hopeless nature must have been obvious to everyone, yet it was carried on vigorously, in the evident determination that no effort should be spared in the cause of freeing the ship.

"It was most gratifying to see the splendid state of the health of the party. Sledging and sawing had combined to bring all into the fittest condition—appetites were enormous, spirits never flagged, and it would have been difficult to find a more contented community.

"The men returned to the ship on January 2. On the following day Dr. Wilson and I proceeded to the ice-edge, and camped on the westernmost headland of Erebus Island, which I have called Cape Royds. We found here a new rookery of Adélie penguins, and a number of erratic granite boulders, and decided to remain some days. At this time the ice showed no sign of breaking up; a loose patch lay off its edge, coming and going with wind and tide, but effectually damping the swell.

"On January 5 were were looking to seaward from our tent, when the 'Morning' hove in sight, shortly followed by another ship, for which we were wholly unable to account. After signalling through to the 'Discovery,' and arranging for the transmission of mails, we went aboard the 'Morning,' and soon learnt all the news. I need not say how concerned I was to learn the extensive preparations that had been made for our relief; the letters made it quite clear how this had come about, but it was impossible not to feel the keenest regret that our position should not have been better known and such a large outlay avoided.

"The instructions to abandon the 'Discovery' cast a gloom over the whole ship; the spirit in which they had been issued was understood, but on the spot, face to face with the situation, the ultimate release of the ship appeared a certainty to everyone. There was not one who would not have been prepared to back his opinion by remaining by her, or who did not shrink from the thought of leaving her. Up to this time we had all held optimistic views of our chances of release in the present season. Captain Colbeck's report of a clear sea to the north was also cheering, but towards the last week in January, when there was little change in the ice conditions, all began to grow despondent; it seemed as though the ice were determined to exact its tribute.

"The 'Terra Nova' attempted to butt the ice with a full head of steam, but the result was insignificant; some explosives were tried, but more with the idea of ascertaining the best method of using them than from hope of an effective result. The distance was altogether too great for such attempts.

"To be prepared for all contingencies, I thought it wise to commence the transport of our most valuable effects to the relief ships on January 15. It was arranged that one large tent should be placed and kept half-way between them and the 'Discovery.' The loads were taken to this tent by our own people, and from thence carried on by the sledge teams to the relief ships. The service became so extremely heavy that the parties were obliged to spend each alternate night in the tent, and it was, therefore, only on alternate days that loads were dispatched from the ship. By the end of the month, all collections, registers, instruments, and valuable books had been transported.

"The first general break-up of the ice commenced towards the end of January. A heavy swell entered the strait, and was felt very distinctly on board the 'Discovery.' The ice went out very rapidly, and in large floes, which streamed away into the north-west. The result of our ten days' labour on the saws went out in one large floe. By the end of the month both ships were inside the glacier, eight miles to the north. On February 3, the open water was within six or seven miles of the 'Discovery, but by this time the swell had almost vanished, and the ice was quiescent. If the explosives were to be used, I now thought the distance warranted their trial, and went myself to the relief ships for that purpose. The ice edge now extended in a straight line, approximately east and west, for a distance of six or seven miles, and this broad front was more or less equi-distant from the 'Discovery' at every point. The slight swell that remained formed long cracks from 100 yards to 200 yards apart, parallel to the ice-edge, and extending its whole length. In course of time a lateral track would suddenly spread from the edge to the outer crack, then in a very short time all the ice beyond the outer crack would strip away along the whole edge. These lateral cracks formed the lines of weakness, and it was in making them artificially that I hoped for good results from the explosives. A few trials proved so effective, that on February 6 an explosive party was sent from the 'Discovery,' and all available hands from the 'Morning' and 'Terra Nova' were employed in digging holes for the explosion. The holes were made from the eastern extremity of the ice on a line towards the 'Discovery,' and at intervals varied according to circumstances. The thickness, and in places the sodden condition of the ice, made this work most laborious, and I cannot speak too highly of the manner in which the crews of both relief ships stuck to their work. On more than one occasion, when the results warranted, they volunteered to continue throughout the night. Although at times the effects of the explosions were most inspiriting and great advance was made, there were several days when little or no good results appeared to be achieved, and as the season advanced each day became of great importance. On February 10 our prospects did not look bright; but on February 11 another big break-up of the ice occurred, and on February 12 the relief ships were within three miles of the 'Discovery.' Explosions were resumed, and on the morning of February 14 this distance had been reduced to one and a-half mile. At 5 p.m. on the same day another break-up commenced, and the men working on the ice could barely be picked up fast enough. The news quickly spread on board the 'Discovery,'

and all hands were soon assembled on Hut Point. The floes appeared
to break away about as fast as the relief ships could steam through
them. As usual, the broken ice streamed away to the north-west.
A large pool of broken water had been gradually forming throughout
the season off Hut Point, and at 11 p.m. the last strip of fast ice
between this pool and the sea broke away, and, amid much enthusiasm, the relief ships steamed round the point and secured abreast
of the 'Discovery.' Although the ice continued to break away to
the south, it held fast in the small bay in which the 'Discovery'
lay, and here it was from 12 feet to 17 feet thick. On February 15
we were busily engaged in filling the boilers. In the night I exploded
a charge, which cracked the floe in all directions.

"Early on February 16, a final explosion practically cleared
our small bay of ice, and the 'Discovery' swung slowly round to
her anchors, one of which was immediately weighed. In the evening
the 'Terra Nova' came alongside to give us coal, but later it blew
hard from the south-west, and she again put to sea. A strong wind
from this quarter was a most rare occurrence, and I expected that,
as usual, the wind would quickly shift to the east; but, though it
lulled in the night, in the morning it increased to a full gale without
change of direction and with a rising sea. The 'Discovery' has
heavy anchor gear, but I knew the holding-ground to be bad, and
that we were too close to the ice-foot to allow of cable being veered.
Steam was raised with all despatch, but before the engines were
ready the ship began to drag, until her stern was bumping against
the ice-foot, and the moment that the engines were reported ready,
I had no option but to weigh anchor. It was an unfortunate
moment for a first trial of the engines, but all would have been well
had we been able to hold our own till clear of the small shoal off
Hut Point, barely a quarter of a mile from the ship. At first we
did so, but later the strong current running to the northward round
this point caught our bows and swept us on to the shoal, and she
took the ground at 11 a.m., with wind, sea, and current all tending
to place her farther ashore. In the afternoon it blew very hard,
the ship bumped very heavily, and the seas broke over her. Knowing
the shoals to be small, and finding a deeper sounding at the bow-
sprit end, I tried with steam and sail to force her over the bank,
but this only seemed to make matters worse. There was nothing to
be done till the weather moderated. It was a very trying time,
but everyone behaved admirably, and arrangements for lightening
the ship were discussed. At 6 p.m. the wind commenced to lull, and
shortly after seven the ship was reported to be forging astern; in a
few minutes there was no doubt of the fact. The engines were put
full steam astern, and the ship rolled, until at 7.30 she slid off into
deep water. Whilst ashore a good deal of the false keel was ripped

off. Beyond this, I do not think the ship sustained any damage whatever. There was no increase in the leaks."

Continuing his narrative, he says: "On March 4, a fairly good haul was made with the trawl. On this day I was much tempted to continue in a south-westerly direction, but had again to deplore the insufficiency of our coal supply. We had now little more than fifty tons left, and this, I knew, would be barely enough to carry us to the rendezvous. The 'Discovery' is a wretched sailer, and in her present trim, with the small spare rudder, is almost unmanageable under sail alone, however the yards may be trimmed. When close hauled she carries almost full weather helm, and makes from three to four points to leeway. To economise coal we had to remain under sail on more than one occasion when amongst bergs, and the situation was rendered more unpleasant by the fact that there were only four hands in the deck watch. Under steam and sail she behaves exceptionally well for a ship of her class; she is very stiff and weatherly, and we have never yet found it necessary to heave to.

"On March 5 we re-crossed the Antarctic Circle, after an interval of two years and two months. From this time we had almost continuous north-westerly and westerly gales until we arrived at Auckland Island. The three days were spent under sail alone, but we made so much leeway that we were obliged to get up steam again. We sighted these islands on March 14, having been close hauled throughout. Early on March 15 we anchored in Laurie Cove, with ten tons of coal remaining in the bunker. The 'Terra Nova' arrived on March 19, and the 'Morning' on March 23. Both ships had experienced very severe weather; they had been driven far to the eastward, and had been repeatedly hove-to. We have here re-filled our boilers, and received thirty-three tons of coal from the "Terra Nova." The 'Morning' is taking in ballast, after which we shall leave for Lyttelton in company.

"I would only at present notice in general terms the conduct of the officers and men of this ship throughout the expedition. I have given my reason for touching lightly on the scientific work accomplished, believing that each officer will receive full credit for his departmental labours, especially under the arrangements which have been made with regard to the scientific publications. But in Polar expedition there must always be times when all must work for the common good regardless of department; at such times there has been no need to ask for volunteers in the "Discovery. On the sledges or on the saws, in coaling or watering the ship, or at any task that needed to be done hurriedly, officers and men have worked alike, and grudged no labour till the work was finished. The conduct of the men has been beyond praise. By them the monotony of the second winter was met with unfailing cheerfulness. Most arduous sledge journeys and the most severe weather were encountered in the same spirit, and with an intelligence that freed the officers from all anxiety as to their welfare. But the qualities of the ship's company have never been more evident than since our release from the ice. The difficulties I have mentioned, and many others which might naturally be expected after such a long captivity in the ice, were overcome only by incessant labour. It was, in the sailor's expression, " Watch, and stop on "; and though many were almost worn out with fatigue, there was neither complaint nor demur when a fresh task was imposed. I shall hope to make their services better known to you on the return of the expedition. Although, as was shown, our small company were so thoroughly able to take care of themselves, and naturally felt some embarrassment at the extent of the relief expedition, I would not have it appear that we under-value the services of the relief ships. Everything that could possibly be done for us they were only too willing to do. Captain Colbeck's arrangements with regard to stores, etc., appear to have been excel-lent, and this year, as last, he has shown himself ever ready to sacrifice his own interests to ours. His conduct of the relief expedi-tion deserves the thanks of his former as well as his present employers. His services were ably seconded by those of Captain M'Kay, of the ' Terra Nova.' Of the officers and crews of both ships, I can only add that I believe they were almost as anxious as ourselves to see the ' Discovery ' released, and almost as pleased when that event was happily accomplished."

Says Sir Clements Markham :

" I believe that the great success of the expedition is due to the command being entrusted to a young naval officer in the regular line, supported by thirty naval officers and men zealously devoted to duty, and resolved to uphold the credit of our noble profession in the far south. The Navy, assuredly, has cause to be proud of their exploring detachment, the names of the officers and men com-posing which will be handed down to future fame. You are aware that the Society is presenting Captain Scott with a special gold medal, and also that our Gracious Sovereign has ordered a medal to be struck in commemoration of the great work which has been achieved. The results of their observations will not be available probably for some years, as it will require a special band of scientists to work up the data thus provided. A committee of the Royal Society has undertaken the magnetic work ; the Royal Geographical Society has undertaken the expenses connected with the meteoro-logical observations ; and the trustees of the British Museum have undertaken to organise and publish the biological and geological results. You are all aware that the ' Discovery ' has reached Eng-land, and that Captain Scott is receiving the thanks and praises which he deserves at the hands of his countrymen."

PROCEEDINGS

OF THE

Royal Geographical Society of Australasia,

QUEENSLAND.

[Unless otherwise stated, all the meetings have been held at the Rooms of the Society, Public Library Building, William Street, Brisbane].

OCTOBER 19th, 1903

THE PRESIDENT, Right Hon. Sir Hugh M. Nelson, K.C.M.G., D.C.L., in the chair.

Messrs. R. E. O'Hara (proposed by Mr. S. Hannaford), David Benjamin (proposed by the Hon. Secretary), G. H. Buzacott (proposed by the President), were elected ordinary members, and Mr. A. A. Lewis (proposed by the Hon. Secretary) was elected a life member of the Society.

THE HON. F. T. BRENTNALL, M.L.C., read a paper on "The Mystery of Ancient Ophir," with lantern slide illustrations. (See Page 1.)

The vote of thanks to the author of the paper was proposed by the President, and carried by acclamation.

OCTOBER 30th, 1903.

This was a provincial meeting, held at the Town Hall, Toowoomba, on the invitation of the Municipality and of the Austral Association.

THE PRESIDENT, Right Hon. Sir Hugh M. Nelson, K.C.M.G., D.C.L., in the chair.

Messrs. R. Billington (proposed by Mr. A. Muir), Alexander Mayes (proposed by the Hon. Secretary, Dr. J. P. Thomson). Hon. E. D. Miles, M.L.C. (proposed by the President, Right Hon. Sir Hugh M. Nelson), Messrs. John H. Munro (proposed by Mr. James Tolmie, M.L.A.), R. H. Munro (proposed by Mr. E. A. Gaden), and Rev. James Stewart (proposed by Mr. James Tolmie) were elected ordinary members of the Society.

MR. JAMES TOLMIE, M.L.A., read a paper on the "Early History of Toowoomba," illustrated by maps. (See Page 18.)

The vote of thanks to the author of the paper was moved by the Hon. F. T. Brentnall, M.L.C., seconded by Mr. A. Muir, and carried unanimously. The meeting stood adjourned till the following day, at the same place. In the meantime, the members of the Society were entertained at a conversazione in the Masonic Hall by the Austral Association, and on the following morning they were shown round the district and town by the Mayor, Alderman A. Mayes, and Messrs. J. Tolmie and J. H. Munro, who were extremely kind and hospitable. In the afternoon the President and Lady Nelson entertained the members of the Society and their friends at an "at home" at "Gabbinbar," which was greatly enjoyed. At the reassembling of the Society in the evening the President re-delivered his address on "Antarctic Exploration and Discovery," with beautiful lantern-slide pictures.

The vote of thanks to the President was moved by Mr. Tolmie, seconded by Mr. R. B. Taylor, and carried by acclamation.

The cordial thanks of the Society was conveyed to His Worship the Mayor and to the Austral Association for hospitality received.

DECEMBER 22nd, 1903.

THE PRESIDENT, Right Hon. Sir Hugh M. Nelson, K.C.M.G., D.C.L., F.R.G.S., in the chair.

On behalf of the Society, the PRESIDENT, congratu ated the Hon. Sir A. C. Gregory, K.C.M.G., on the honour of Knighthood recently conferred upon him by the King.

In the name of the Council, Fellows, and Members of the Society, the VICE-PRESIDENT, Hon. Arthur Morgan, M.L.A., congratulated the President on his election as a Fellow of the Royal Geographical Society, London.

THE HON. JOHN DOUGLAS, C.M.G., F.R.G.S., read a paper on "The Maritime Boundary of Queensland," illustrated by a map. (See Page 32.)

The vote of thanks to the author of the paper was moved by the Right Hon. Sir S. W. Griffith, seconded by Sir A. C. Gregory, and carried unanimously.

APRIL 28th, 1904.

THE PRESIDENT, Right Hon. Sir Hugh M. Nelson, K.C.M.G., D.C.L., F.R.G.S., in the chair.

Mr. W. H. Gaden was elected an ordinary member of the Society, on the nomination of the President and Mr. John Cameron, M.L.A.

An improved Mountain Aneroid Barometer, made in London to the order of the President, was handed round the room for inspection.

MR. GEORGE WOOLNOUGH, M.A., read a paper on "New Zealand: Its Geographical and Meteorological Conditions considered in their bearing on Field Industries." The paper was illustrated by two wall maps. (See Page 37.)

The vote of thanks to the author of the paper was moved by Mr. John Cameron, M.L.A., seconded by Mr. R. M. Collins, supported by Mr. E. E. Edwards, B.A., and carried.

JUNE 23rd, 1904.

THE HON. F. T. BRENTNALL, M.L.C., in the chair.

Messrs. P. W. Crowe and C. F. Buderus were elected ordinary members of the Society, on the nomination of Messrs. Alexr. Muir and R. Fraser.

Dr. W. E. ROTH, B.A., delivered an address, with numerous lantern-slide illustrations, on "The Every-day Life of the North Queensland Blacks."

THE HON. J. F. G. FOXTON, M.L.A., made some interesting remarks on the subject of the address, after which the meeting accorded the lecturer a vote of thanks by acclamation.

ANNUAL GENERAL MEETING.

SEPTEMBER 19th, 1904.

THE PRESIDENT, Right Hon. Sir Hugh M. Nelson, K.C.M.G., D.C.L., F.R.G.S., in the chair.

Miss Alice J. Alison-Greene was elected an ordinary member of the Society, on the nomination of the Hon. F. T. Brentnall, M.L.C.

THE HON. SECRETARY, Dr. J. P. Thomson, read the Council's Report, and THE HON. TREASURER, Mr. D. S. Thistlethwayte, submitted the Financial Statement, both of which were adopted, on the motion of the Hon. F. T. Brentnall, seconded by Mr. John Cameron. M.L.A.

THE PRESIDENT then delivered the anniversary address, on the subject of the work of the British National Expedition to the Antarctic regions and the return of Captain Scott. (See Page 73.)

The vote of thanks to the President for his interesting and instructive address was moved by the Hon. J. T. Bell, M.L.A. (Minister for Lands), and seconded by Mr. J. G. McDonald, F.R.G.S.

The Officers and Council were re-elected for the session 1904-05, as follows :— President : The Right Hon. Sir Hugh M. Nelson, K.C.M.G., D.C.L., F.R.G.S. Vice-President : Hon. Arthur Morgan, M.L.A. Hon. Treasurer : D. S. Thistlethwayte, C.E. Hon. Secretary : J. P. Thomson, LL.D., Hon. F.R.S.G.S., Etc.

Council for 1904-1905.—Robert Fraser, F.R.G.S.A.Q., Lieut-Col. J. Irving, M.R.C.V.S.L., A. S. Kennedy, C. B. Lethem, C. E.. G. Phillips, C.E., John Cameron, M.L.A., Hon. F. T. Brentnall, M.L.C., F. L. Schoenheimer, J.P., Hon. Auditor : C. W. de Vis, M.A.

The meeting afterwards adjourned for light refreshments.

ROYAL GEOGRAPHICAL SOCIETY OF AUSTRALASIA, QUEENSLAND.

REPORT OF COUNCIL.

NINETEENTH SESSION, 1903-1904.

In submitting the Nineteenth Annual Report on the operations of the Society during the preceding session, the Council notes with pleasure the satisfactory nature of the work performed, and the continued interest evinced by the Members and public in the meetings held from time to time.

Fifteen candidates have been elected to the ordinary membership during the session, the total number of Members on the roll being 260, of whom eighteen are of the Honorary and Corresponding class.

The Council has to record with very deep regret the death of the Hon. John Douglas, who was one of the first Honorary Members, being a highly-valued contributor to the Society's literature, a warm exponent of the Society's objects, and one of the pioneer statesmen of Queensland. There has also occurred the death of Major J. W. Powell, Director of the Bureau of American Ethnology, a valued Corres-

ponding Member; and of Mr. F. W. Hardcastle, of Wyndham,
Western Australia, one of the oldest Life Members of the Society.
These losses are much deplored.

The Hon. Treasurer's statement of accounts, submitted herewith,
discloses the current financial affairs of the Society.

Whilst acknowledging with cordial thanks the many valuable
additions to the Library from kindred institutions the world over,
the Council desires to especially mention an acceptable gift of thirty
books of geography and travel from the President, Right Hon. Sir
Hugh M. Nelson, K.C.M.G., to whom the Society is greatly indebted.

Volume eighteen of the "Journal" was sent out to Members
and "Exchanges" in the usual way, and was generally acknowledged
to be one of the most interesting numbers ever issued by the Society.
In this connection, it is very satisfactory to note the increasing
demand for our publications, as affording evidence of the development of the geographical work of the State.

The papers read during the session are printed in this issue of
the "Journal," and although not very numerous are of wide interest
in the variety of subjects with which they deal.

The Council considers that the papers received in competition
for the Society's Thomson Foundation Gold Medal do not sufficiently
comply with the conditions laid down by the Society, and there will
in consequence be no award of the Medal this session.

The Council again recommends:—(1) The suspension of so much
of the Rules as provides for the payment of an entrance fee; (2) the
re-appointment of Sir A. C. Gregory and Messrs. Alex. Muir and
C. W. de Vis as Hon. Councillors and Referees.

The Hon. Secretary, Dr. J. P. Thomson, has resumed his duties
after an interesting and useful tour round the world, an account of
which in book form has been published under the auspices of the
President and Council of this Society.

BALANCE SHEET, 1903–1904.

THE ROYAL GEOGRAPHICAL SOCIETY OF AUSTRALASIA, QUEENSLAND.

Dr.

	£	s.	d.
By Balance brought forward—			
Royal Bank	16	2	6
Government Savings Bank	48	17	8
,, Annual Subscriptions	109	2	0
,, Government Grant	50	0	0
,, Interest on Government Savings Bank Deposit ..	1	8	9
	£225	**10**	**11**

Cr.

	£	s.	d.	£	s.	d.
To Expenditure as per accounts—						
Printing, Stationery, Postage, &c.	123	3	6			
Advertising, Reporting, &c. ..	2	4	9			
Fire Insurance, Rent of Safe, &c.	3	17	3			
Gas Account	1	3	1			
Sundry Expenses, Meetings, &c. ..	16	4	1			
				146	12	8
,, Bank Charges for Keeping Account ..				0	10	0
,, Exchanges, etc.				0	9	8
				147	11	11
,, Balance in Royal Bank				27	12	7
,, Balance in Government Savings Bank..				50	6	5
				£225	**10**	**11**

Examined with Bank Pass Book, Vouchers, &c., and found correct.

C. W. DE VIS, *Auditor.*

Brisbane, July 15th, 1904.

D. S. THISTLETHWAYTE, *Hon. Treasurer.*

Adopted—HUGH M. NELSON, 19/9/04.

Royal Geographical Society of Australasia,

QUEENSLAND.

DIPLOMAS OF FELLOWSHIP.

The following gentlemen have been awarded the Diploma of Fellowship under Section IV. of Clause 8, Constitution and Rules (*See page 2 of cover*) :—

Honorary :

His Excellency Sir William MacGregor, K.C.M.G., C.B., M D., D.Sc., Hon. F.R.S.G.S., etc.

Hon. Sir A. C. Gregory, K.C.M.G., F.R.G.S., Hon.F.R.S.G.S., M.L.C., etc.

The Right Hon. Lord Lamington, G.C.M.G., B.A., F.R.G.S., Hon. F.R.S.G.S., etc

Under subsections (a and b) :—

Lieut.-Col. James Irving, P.V.O., Q.D.F., M.R.C.V.S.L.

J. A. Baxendell, Esq.

William Jones, Esq., J.P.

Charles Battersby, Esq., J.P.

Robert Fraser, Esq., J P.

Rev. W. M. Walsh, P.P.

E. M. Waraker, Esq.

R. M. Collins, Esq., J.P.

Alexander Muir, Esq., J.P.

C. B. Lethem, Esq., C.E.

D. S. Thistlethwayte, Esq., C.E

LIST OF MEMBERS.

(P) Members who have contributed papers which are published in the Society's "Proceedings and Transactions." The numerals indicate the number of such contributions.

(PP) Past President.

A dagger (†) prefixed to a name indicates a member of the Council.

Life members are distinguished thus (*).

Should any error or omission be found in this list, it is requested that notice thereof be given to the Hon. Secretary.

Foundation Members :

Atkinson, J. R., J.P., Lic. Surveyor, Ipswich, Queensland.

Daniell, E. N., ———

Gailey, R , J.P., Courier Building, Brisbane.

P9PP †Gregory, Hon. Sir A.C., K.C.M.G., F.R.G.S , M.L.C., etc., Mary Street, Brisbane.

Marks, Hon. C. F., M.D., M.L.C., Wickham Terrace, Brisbane.

P1 *Moor, T. B., F.R.G.S., F.R.S. Tas., Strahan, West Coast, Tasmania.

P1 †Muir, A., J.P., F.R.G.S.A.Q., Queen Street, Brisbane.

P33PP †Thomson, J. P , LL.D., Hon.F.R.S.G.S., etc., Hon. Secretary, Wood Street, South Brisbane.

Members :

Affleck, Thos. H., "West Hall," Freestone, Warwick, Queensland.

Ahern, John, L.S., Charters Towers, Queensland.

Aldridge, H. E., J.P., "Baddow," Maryborough, Queensland

Alison-Greene, Miss Alice J., Moreton Bay Girls' High School, Wynnum.

Alton, Ralph, Nelson Street, South Brisbane.

Archibald, The Hon. John, M.L.C., "Glenugie," New Farm, Brisbane.

Armstrong, L., J.P., Normanton, Queensland.

Ashmole, Arthur, "Ilford House," Redcliffe, Queensland.

Bartholomew, T., J.P., Woombye, North Coast Line, Queensland.

Barton, E. J. T., "Courier" Office, Brisbane.

Barton. E. C., Electrical Supply Co., Ann Street, Brisbane.

Battersby, C., J.P., F.R.G.S.A.Q., Georgetown, Queensland.

Baxendell, J. A., F.R.G.S.A.Q., Downs Grammar School, Toowoomba.

Bean, J. H., J.P., Gasworks, Cairns, Queensland.

Beit, William, J.P., "Ascot," Toowoomba, Queensland.

Bembrick, Rev. M. L., Lufilufi, Samoa.

Benjamin, D.. Breakfast Creek Road, Brisbane.

Bernays, L. A., C.M.G., F.L.S., Parliament House, Brisbane.

Bell, John, Merchant, Elizabeth Street, Brisbane.

Bell, Hon. J. T., M.L.A , Minister for Public Lands, Brisbane.

B.I. and Q.A. Coy. (The Manager), Mary Street, Brisbane.

Bonar, W. M., J.P., Herberton, Queensland.

Borton, Mark W., Lands Office, Barcaldine, Queensland.

P1 † Brentnall. Hon. F. T , M.L.C., Coorparoo, Brisbane

Brier, James F., "Royston," Albion.

* Bright, Allan B., J.P., Charters Towers, Queensland.

Bright, C. E., Inspector Post and Telegraph Dept., Brisbane, Queensland.

Brown, D. L., J.P., Bala Hills, near Brisbane.

Brown, Isaac, J., J.P., Maytown, Queensland.

Broadbent, Kendall, Museum, Brisbane.

Buzacott, G. H., Deputy P.M.G., Post Office, Brisbane.

Callan, Hon. A. J., M.L.C., "Marie Villa," Mayne, near Brisbane.

† Cameron, John, M.L.A., Courier Building, Brisbane.

Cameron, W., Geological Survey Office, Brisbane.

Cameron, Charles Christopher, "Coolabah," Ipswich.

* Campbell, A., J.P., Glengyle Station, Birdsville, Queensland.

Carter, Hon. A. J., M.L.C., Royal Swedish and Norwegian Consulate, 35 Eagle Street, Brisbane.

P1 Charlton, F. J., Staff Surveyor, Survey Office, Brisbane.

Chermside, His Excellency Major-General Sir Herbert, G.C.M.G., C.B. (Patron).

Christensen, J., ————

Clark, James, J.P., "Wybenia," New Farm, Brisbane.

Clerk, E. G., junr., Malboona, Corfield, Queensland.

Coakes, W. J., Messrs. Finney, Isles and Co., Brisbane.

P2PP * Collins, R. M., J.P., F.R.G.S.A.Q., Tamrookum, Beaudesert, Queensland.

Corrie, Alderman Leslie G., J.P., F.L.S., Edward Street, Brisbane.

Costin, C. W., Parliament House, Brisbane.

P2 Cox, W. G., C.E., 16 West Park Gardens, Kew, London, England.

Coxen, Henry William, J.P., "The Fort," Oxley, near Brisbane.

Craig, Robert, J.P., Cairns, Queensland.

Cullen, Mrs. M. L., "Ardendeuchar," Warwick, Queensland.

Cribb, Hon. Thos. B., M.L.A., Ipswich, Queensland.

Crompton, Wm. Lee, c/o. Agent-General for Queensland, London, England.

* Crorkan, T., J.P., ————

Crowe, P. W., Darragh's Buildings, 170a Queen Street, Brisbane.

Cunningham, J. S., Mundingburra, Townsville, Queensland.

Cunningham, M. W., J.P., Rannes, River Dee, via Rockhampton, Queensland.

Curtis, Lieut., G. A. H., R.N.R., "Gayundah," Brisbane.

Davies, Alderman John, J.P., West End Pharmacy, S. Brisbane, Queensland.

De Vaux, W. R., Birdsville, Queensland.

P1 † De Vis, C. W., M.A., Museum, Brisbane.

Dorph, W.P F., M.R.A.S., Hon Sec. for N.S W. Palestine Exploration Fund, Moore Theological College, Newtown, Sydney, N.S.W.

Dunsmure, Fred., J.P., "Eurella," Roma, Queensland.

Earle, Horace, Johnsonian Club, Brisbane, Queensland.

Edkins, E. R., J.P., Mount Cornish, Muttaburra, Queensland.

Edwards, Edward E., B.A., "Bryntirion," Wickham Terrace, Brisbane.

Eggar, G. W., Survey Office, Brisbane.

P1 Embley, J. T., Lic. Sur., c/o. Survey Office, Brisbane.

Finlay, Miss Laura Lucie, 17 Craven Hill Gardens, Hyde Park, London.

Ferguson, Hon. John, M.L.C, Senator, Rockhampton, Queensland.

Fish, Alderman George South Brisbane

Fisher, Surgeon Walter, J.F., Q.M.D.F., "Shanakeel," Main Street, South Brisbane.

Fleming, Peter, Junr., Brighton Road, South Brisbane.

Fletcher, Victor O., J.P., ————, Queensland.

* Foot, J. A., J.P., Warrinilla, Rolleston, Queensland

Forrest, J. H., J.P., ————, Sydney, N S.W.

Forrest, Hon. E. B., M.L.A., Messrs. Parbury and Co., Eagle Street, Brisbane.

Forster, C. E., J.P., Goondi, Johnstone River, Queensland.

Fox, G., M.L.A., Parliament House, Brisbane.

Frackelton, Rev. W. S., Ph.D., etc., Presbyterian Manse, Ann Street. Brisbane.

† Fraser, Robert, F.R.G.S.A.Q., J.P., Charlotte Street, Brisbane.

Fullerton, Alex. Young, B.A., L.R.C.P., M.R.C.S., ———

Gaden, E. A., J.P., Queensland Club, Brisbane.

Gilligan, John, Parliament House, Brisbane.

Gregory, Edmund, J.P., Petrie Terrace, Brisbane.

Pl PP Griffith, Rt. Hon. Sir S. W., G.C.M.G., M.A., etc., Brisbane.

Grimani-Smith, H. W., J.P., Canmaroo Station, Dalby, Queensland

Gross, Capt. G., Boys' Grammar School, Brisbane.

Hamley, Henry Hubert, Sandgate, Queensland.

Hannaford, S., J.P., Marble Hills, Glenlyon, Stanthorpe, Queensland.

Harbord, H. H., J.P., Maytown, Queensland.

Heindorff, H., Messrs. Heindorff Bros., Queen Street, Brisbane.

Heindorff, W., Messrs. Heindorff Bros., Queen Street, Brisbane.

Hemmy, H. J., L.S., Kwala, Lumpor, Salangor, Straits Settlement.

Hertzberg, A. M., J.P., Hertzberg and Co., Charlotte Street, Brisbane.

Hillcoat, Reginald E. R., J.P., Boomarra Station, via Donaldson, Q'land

Pl Hirschfeld, Eugen, M.D., etc., Wickham Terrace, Brisbane.

* Hodel, F. C., J.P., Thursday Island, Torres Strait, Queensland.

Hogarth, Mrs. William, Balgownie, Cambooya, Q.

Holberton, Hon. F. H., M.L.C., Toowoomba, Queensland.

* Holt, W. H., F.R.C.I., "Glanwyne," Manly Point, Manly, N.S.W.

Horsman, T. P., J.P., Terra Mellis, Pinbarren Siding, N.C.R., Q'land.

Huet, F. A., Queen Street, Brisbane.

Hughes, J., J.P., Income Tax Commissioner, William Street, Brisbane.

Hughes, E. F., Dental Rooms, Treasury Chambers, George Street, Bris.

Hutchinson, L. H., Post Office, Albion.

Hutton, G. S., J.P., Eagle Street, Brisbane.

Innes, S. N., L.S., Cresswell Downs, Camooweal, Queensland.

† Irving, Lieut.-Col. J., M.R.C.V.S.L., J.P., F.R.G.S.A.Q., Ann Street, Brisbane.

Jolliffe, Edwin Alfred, J.P., "Florence Villa," Hamilton.

Jones, Ald. Wm., J.P., F.R.G.S.A.Q., Stephens Street, South Brisbane.

Jones, E. R. ———

Kellaway, Edwin B., Commission Agent, etc., Queen Street, Brisbane

Kemp, John, City Engineer, Town Hall, Brisbane.

Kenealy, P., Albion, Brisbane.

† Kennedy, A. S., Hon. Librarian, Kingsholme, Fortitude Valley, Brisbane.

Kennedy, Thomas, J.P., Allora, Queensland

Kelly-Cusack, William George, P.M., etc., Ravenswood, Queensland.

Klugh, C. R., J.P., Longreach, Queensland.

Pl Lamington, The Right Hon. Lord, G.C.M.G., etc., Government House, Bombay, India.

Lang, Alderman John, Cordelia Street, South Brisbane.

Leahy, Hon. J., M.L.A., Brisbane.

Lee-Bryce, R., J.P., Elizabeth Street, Brisbane.

Lees, Wm., City Printing Works, Queen Street, Brisbane.

† Lethem, C. B., C. E., F.R.G.S.A.Q., Clayfield, Brisbane.

* Lewis, A. A , J.P., Oxley, near Brisbane.

Macartney, J. A., J.P., F.R.G.S., Queensland Club, Brisbane (also Diamantina Lakes).

Macdonald, A. B., J.P., Grosvenor Downs, Clermont, Queensland.

MacDonald, J. G., P.M., F.R.G.S., South Brisbane.

Macdonald-Paterson, Hon. T., Brisbane.

MacGillivray, A. S., J.P.,————

MacGinley, J. J., Bacteriological Institute, Brisbane.

Macintosh, H., Survey Office. Brisbane.

Macansh, Thos. W., Wantley Street, Warwick, Queensland.

Mackie, R. Cliffe, River View Terrace. Hamilton.

P2 Maguire, H. R., L.S., c/o Survey Office, Perth, W. Australia.

May, T. H., M.D., L.S.A., Bundaberg, Queensland.

Mayes, Alderman Alexander, Toowoomba, Q.

* Mathieson, John, Midland Railway, Derby, England.

Matthews, G. S., Imperial Insurance Co., Queen Street, Brisbane.

* McConnel, J. H., J.P., Cressbrook, Queensland.

McDonald-Terry, A. J., J.P., Kirknie Station, Clare, *via* Townsville,

McGroarty, D. C., Jane Street, West End, South Brisbane.

McIver, I. I., J.P., Bulgroo, Adavale, Queensland.

Midson, Arthur, Edmondstone Street, South Brisbane.

Miles, Hon. E. D., M.L.C.. New Farm. Brisbane.

Miller, Ernest H., Solicitor, School of Arts, Ipswich, Queensland.

Minto, A. T., Royal Insurance Coy., Queen Street, Brisbane.

P1 † Morgan, The Hon. Arthur, M.L.A., Vice-President, "Acacia House," Warwick, Queensland.

Moreton, The Hon. B. B., M.L.C., South Australian Mortgage Coy., Adelaide Street, Brisbane.

Moran, R. W.,————

Morris, R., Parliament House, Brisbane.

Müller, Edmund, 118 Elizabeth Street, Brisbane.

Munro, Jas., J.P., Webster and Co., Mary Street, Brisbane

Munro, J. H., "Ness Bank," Toowoomba.

Murray, C. W., J.P., Hughenden, Queensland.

Musgrave, Hon. A., M.L.C., Port Moresby, British New Guinea.

Mylne, Thomas, Glenelg Street, South Brisbane.

Myles, G. T., Palmerin Street, Warwick, Queensland.

P6 † Nelson, His Excellency the Right Hon. Sir Hugh M., K.C.M.G., D.C.L., F.R.G.S., President, Legislative Council, Brisbane.

Needham, F. H., Canning Downs, Warwick, Queensland.

Neilson, R. D.. Indooroopilly.

Nicholas, H. C. R., J.P., Mt. Chalmer Copper Mines, Ltd., Rockhampton.

Nicholas, C. E., Mine Office, North Lyell, Tasmania.

Noble. John James, M.A.,————

Outridge, P. P., Redland Bay, Queensland.

O'Donohue, M., C.P.S., Bowen, Queensland.

O'Hara, R. E., Glenelg, Warwick, Q.

O'Reilly, Charles, Dornoch Terrace, South Brisbane.

O'Shea, Miss E., "Middenbury," Toowong, Brisbane.

Paine, A. A., J.P., Brandon, *via* Townsville. Queensland.

* Parker, Francis, J.P., St. Albans, *via* Monkira, Queensland.

Parr. Mrs. B. C., "Mai Gunyah," Warwick, Queensland.

Pasco, M. G. C., Bank of Australasia, Toowoomba, Queensland.

Peek. F. W., J.P., Ferndale, Loganholme, Queensland.

Pennefather, C. E. de F., Prisons Department, Brisbane.

Petrie, Andrew Lang, M.L.A., Toowong, near Brisbane, Queensland.

† Phillips, George, C.E., Telegraph Chambers, Queen Street, Brisbane.

* Plant, Major C. F., F.R.A.S., "Ferndale," Ashgrove, near Brisbane.

Potts, John, J.P., Sandgate, Q.

Quaid, J. D., J.P., 101 Queen Street, Brisbane, Queensland.

Queale, Robert, J.P., Dornoch Terrace, South Brisbane, Queensland.

Radcliffe, O., Inspector of Schools, Maryborough, Queensland.

Raff, Alex. C., C.E., Railway Offices, Roma Street, Brisbane.

Raff, Hon. Alexander, M.L.C., Gregory Terrace, Brisbane, Queensland.

Ralston, W. V., J.P., Queensland National Bank, Brisbane.

Robertson, J. A., J.P., Bowen Hills, Brisbane.

Rutlidge, Charles Schaefer, c/o Wm. Schaefer, Esq., 12 Wallace Road, London, N.

Rigby, W. A., J.P., South British Ins. Coy., Queen Street, Brisbane.

† Schoenheimer, L. F., J.P., "Val-Myr," Gray Road, South Brisbane.

Scott, W. J., Under Secretary, Lands Department, Brisbane.

Sinclair, J. M., Stephens Street, South Brisbane.

Slade, W. B., Glengallan, Warwick, Queensland.

Sorell, John Arnold, ———

St. Ledger, A. J., Celtic Chambers, Brisbane.

Spiers, James, Toowoomba, Queensland.

Starcke, A., Land Commissioner, Rockhampton.

Steuart, A., Queensland National Bank, Brisbane.

* Stevens, Hon. E. J., M.L.C., Southport, Queensland.

Stewart, Rev. James, Murphy's Creek, Queensland.

Stodart, James, M.L.A., Market Street, Brisbane.

Stopford, W. E. ———

Strathdee, Robert, "Maudsleigh," Bundaberg, Queensland.

Sword, T. S., J.P., Land Board, Brisbane.

* Taylor, W. B., "Blackdown House," Toowoomba, Queensland.

Thallon, J. F., J.P., Eagle Junction, Brisbane.

P3 † Thistlethwayte, D. S., C.E., F.R.G.S.A.Q., Hon. Treasurer, Clayfield, Brisbane.

* Thomas, J. S., "Eblana," Penkivil Street, Bondi, Sydney, N.S.W.

Thomas, Hon. Lewis, M.L.C., "Brynhyfryd," Ipswich, Queensland.

Thomson, A. A., c/o Tattersall's Club, Sydney.

P4 Thomson, Capt. W. C., Swan Hill, Brisbane.

Tolmie, J., M.L.A., Toowoomba.

Trouton, W. J., J.P., Queen Street, Brisbane.

Uhr, John Frederick, J.P., —— Queensland.

Waddell, W. A., Koorboora, via Cairns, Queensland.

Walker, Edgar W., J.P., New Zealand Ins. Co., Queen Street, Brisbane.

Walsh, A. D., Dalgety and Co., Elizabeth Street, Brisbane.

* Walsh, Rev. W. M., P.P., St. Joseph's, Townsville, Queensland.

Walsh, Nugent, c/o Robertson, Tait and Co., Adelaide St., Brisbane.

Waraker, E. M., J.P., F.R.G.S.A.Q., Staff Surveyor, Survey Office, Brisbane.

Watts, J., "Ardoyne," Corinda, near Brisbane.

* Weedon, W., General Post Office, Brisbane.

* Weedon, S. H., C.E., L.S., Box 44, G.P.O., Sydney, N.S.W.

Welsby, Thomas, Darragh's Buildings, Queen Street, Brisbane.

P1 Williams, Capt. J., c/o Burns, Philp and Co., Sydney, N.S.W.

Williams, Sidney, J.P., Rockhampton, Queensland.

Wilson, Hon. A. Heron, M.L.C., Maryborough, Queensland.

Wilson, W. A., J.P., Fernvale, c/o Messrs. B. G. Wilson and Co., Queen Street, Brisbane.

P 1 Winter, Sir F. P., Kt., ———

Wyatt, W. H., J.P., ———

Honorary Members :

Lady Norman, Royal Hospital, Chelsea, London, S.W., England.

The Right Hon. Lord Stanmore, G.C.M.G., etc., House of Lords, London, England.

H.I.H. Prince Roland Bonaparte, 10 Avenue d'Iena, Paris, France.

Sir Clements R. Markham, K.C.B.. F.R.S., etc., President, Royal Geo. Soc., 21 Ecclestone Square, London, S.W., England.

Honorary Corresponding Members

His Excellency Sir William MacGregor, K.C.M.G., C.B., M.D., D.Sc., Hon. F.R.S.G.S., etc., Govt. House, St. Johns, Newfoundland.

John Tebbut, Esq., F.R.A.S., etc., etc., Private Observatory, "Peninsula," Windsor, N.S.W.

Charles Gauthiot, Secretaire Generale de la Societe de Geographie Commerciale, Paris.

P1 H. R. Mill, Esq., LL.D., D.Sc. F.R.S.E., F.R.G.S., F.R.S.G.S., Director, British Rainfall Organisation, 62 Camden Square, London, N.W., England.

P1 S. P. Smith, F.R.G.S., New Plymouth, New Zealand.

H. C. Russell, Esq., B.A., C.M.G., F.R.S., F.R.A.S., F.R.Met. Soc., The Observatory, Sydney, N.S.W.

Sir Sandford Fleming, K.C.M.G., LL.D., C.E., Ottawa, Canada.

Hon. W. T. Harris, Ph.D., LL.D., Commissioner of Education, Washington, D.C., U.S.A.

P13 R. H. Mathews, Esq., Assoc. Memb. Soc. d'Anthrop. de Paris ; Corr. Memb. Anthrop. Soc., Washington, "Carcuran," Hassall Street, Parramatta, N.S.W.

Mrs. J. P. Thomson, Wood Street, South Brisbane.

His Excellency Sir G. R. Le Hunte, K.C.M.G., Govt. House, Adelaide.

Dr. Gerard Trower, D.D., Bishop of Likoma, British Central Africa.

His Excellency the Hon. W. L. Allardyce, C M.G., Government House, Stanley, Falkland Islands.

EIGHTH INTERNATIONAL GEOGRAPHIC CONGRESS.

Washington, D.C., October 26th, 1904.

Secretary of Royal Geographical Society, Brisbane, Queensland, Australia.

Dear Sir,—The enclosed resolutions were adopted by the Eighth International Geographic Congress, and to them the Geographical Societies of the world are urged to give wide publicity. I beg, therefore, if practicable, you will find place for them in your journal, and thus aid in the advancement of the wishes of the Congress.

Very respectfully,
HENRY GANNETT,
General Secretary.

RESOLUTIONS ADOPTED BY THE EIGHTH INTERNATIONAL GEOGRAPHIC CONGRESS, SEPTEMBER 13TH, 1904.

RULES FOR GEOGRAPHIC NAMES.

Local names are as far as possible to be preserved, not only in those regions where already established, but also in wild regions. They should on this account be determined with all the accuracy possible.

Where local names do not exist or cannot be discovered, the names applied by the first discoverer should be used until further investigation. The arbitrary altering of historical, long-existent names, well known not only in common use, but also in science, is to be regarded as extremely unadvisable, and every means should be employed to resist such alterations. Inappropriate and fantastical names are to be replaced, as far as possible, by local and more appropriate names.

The above rules are not to be rigorously construed, yet they should be followed to a greater extent than heretofore by travellers and in scientific works. Their publication in periodicals, as the opinion of Congress, will probably prove of great weight. Although in recent years many official systems of determination of geographic names have been enunciated, we have still evidence of the very slight influence which the wishes of the International Geographic Congresses exert over the decision of the official authorities. To this Geographical Societies are urged to give wide publicity.

INTRODUCTION OF THE FRACTIONAL SCALES OF MAPS.

The Seventh International Geographic Congress expressed the urgent wish that upon all charts, including those published by those lands still employing the English and Russian systems of measurement, along with the scale of geographic co-ordinance, that the scale of reduction should be expressed in the usual fractional form, l.x. and that the latter be added to all lists of charts covering land and sea, and requests the Executive Committee of the Congress to bring this decision to the attention of all Governments, Geographical Societies, and establishments engaged in the publication of charts.

The advantage to be derived from the support of this resolution, which has its origin with the editor of Peterman's Mittheilungen and the extensive dissemination of the resolution, is at once evident. In English publications a custom has arisen of adding a statement of the ratio l.x. to the usually employed x-miles to one inch. In America the custom has arisen of going even a step beyond this, namely, the addition of the ratio of reduction has led to the direct application of the decimal system in the units of measure adopted upon the charts. To this Geographical Societies are urged to give wide publicity.

H—ROYAL GEO. SOCIETY.

THE DECIMAL SYSTEM.

The Seventh National Geographic Congress expresses itself in favour of a uniform system in all geographical researches and discussions, and it recommends for this purpose the employment of the metric system of weights and measures, as also the employment of the Centigrade thermometric scale.

It is, moreover, highly desirable that there should always be added to statements of the Fahrenheit, and the Reaumur scales, their equivalent upon the scale of celsias.

Similar is this question of the metric system, which reaches even more deeply than the former into the well-established customs of daily life, and has proved, not without value, in promoting international uniformity and simplicity. Although the metric system of weights and measures has made slow progress, and this alone through the portals of scientific work, its application to geophysics and geography has already made a fair beginning. In England a special organisation, entit'ed the Decimal Association, has taken charge of the matter. The Commonwealth of Australia has entrusted the subject to a commission. We are without knowledge of the efforts iu this direction thus far made in Russia. To this Geographical Societies are urged to give wide publicity.

STANDARD TIME.

Resolved, in view of the fact that a large majority of the nations of the world have already adopted systems of standard time, based upon the Meridian of Greenwich, as prime meridian, that this Congress is in favour of the universal adoption of the Meridian of Greenwich as the basis of all systems of standard time.

PUBLICATION OF PHOTOGRAPHS

It is suggested by the lantern slides shown by Mr. Siebers and by the photographs by Mr. Willis, that it is desirable that in these and the cases of other exploring travellers, photographs of geographical significance might be published, and accompanied by short explanatory notes, so that they may form collections of representative physical features of different parts of the world.

The Royal Geographical Society of Australasia,

QUEENSLAND.

CONDITIONS OF COMPETITION FOR THE THOMSON FOUNDATION GOLD MEDAL.

The Thomson Foundation Gold Medal of this Society will be awarded to the Author of the Best Original Paper (provided it be of sufficient merit) on each of the following subjects :—

To be sent in not later than 1st July, 1905.

1.—THE GEOGRAPHICAL DISTRIBUTION OF AUSTRALIAN MINERALS.

To be sent in not later than 1st July, 1906.

2.—THE AGRICULTURAL INDUSTRY OF AUSTRALIA.

The competition is open to Members and Non-members of the Society alike, whether residing in Australasia or elsewhere, but not to any Officer of the Society or Member of the Council for the time being. No award of the Medal will be made for a mere compilation, no matter how meritorious.

All competitive communications for the Medal should be written on one side of the paper only, with marginal space on the left hand side thereof, and limited to, say, about 32 pages of the "Queensland Geographical Journal," Royal 8vo. Instead of the writer's name each paper must be identified by a motto. A sealed envelope with such motto written outside, and the writer's name and address inside, should accompany each paper.

The successful papers will be printed and published in the Journal of the Society, fifty reprint copies of each being supplied to the author, free.

All communications, with illustrations for which the Medal may be awarded, must be written in the English language, and will become the property of the Society absolutely.

Papers may be illustrated by such maps, diagrams and pictures as are considered by the authors thereof to be necessary and useful.

Additional subjects for future papers will be announced from time to time.

All communications should be addressed to the Hon. Secretary of the Society, Brisbane

HUGH M. NELSON, *President*

J. P. THOMSON, *Hon. Secretary.*

THE THOMSON FOUNDATION GOLD MEDAL

OF

The Royal Geographical Society of Australasia,

QUEENSLAND.

(Established in honour of J. P. Thomson, LL.D., Hon.F.R.S.G.S., etc.,
Founder. See pages 132-135 of Journal, Vol. XVI.)

— ◆◆◆ —

CONDITIONS.

This Medal shall be awarded annually, or at such other times as the Council may approve, to the author of the best original contribution to Geographical Literature, provided it be of sufficient merit, approved and accepted by the Society (the subject of such contribution to be named by the Council). Special awards of the Medal may also be made from time to time to such persons as have gratuitously rendered eminent services to the Society.

The Council may award a silver or a bronze impression of the Medal to the Author of a contribution deemed to further the interests of the Society and add to the value of Geographical Literature.

The Council shall name from time to time the subject of such contribution for which the Medal is to be awarded, preferential consideration being given to the Geography of Australasia.

All contributions for which the Medal may be awarded must be written in the English language, and will become the property of the Society absolutely.

It shall not be competent for any Officer of the Society or Member of the Council for the time being to compete for the Medal.

The administration of the Medal shall be entirely in the hands of the Council of the Society, who will make such additional rules and regulations for awarding the Medal as from time to time may seem necessary.

CPSIA information can be obtained at www.ICGtesting.com
Printed in the USA
BVOW07s1948260514

354513BV00009B/559/P